# GROWING UP
# KARANTH

**Kota Ullas Karanth** was originally trained as an engineer, but pursued his passion for wildlife biology, getting his master's degree at the University of Florida, USA (1988) and doctorate from Mangalore University (1993). Focusing on tiger ecology, Karanth has published over 150 scientific articles, 8 books in English and 4 books in Kannada. He has been recognised by the Fellowship of the Indian Academy of Sciences, and has been awarded the Presidential honour Padma Shri and J. Paul Getty Award from the World Wildlife Fund, USA. He has academic affiliations at the University of Florida, USA and the Tata Institute of Fundamental Research—NCBS, Bengaluru.

**Malavika Kapur** is a visiting professor at the National Institute of Advanced Studies (NIAS) Bengaluru, after retiring as head of the Department of Clinical Psychology at the National Institute of Mental Health and Neurosciences I (NIMHANS). Kapur has published 20 books and over 100 articles and has received the Fellowship of the Indian Association of Clinical Psychologists, Indian Association of Child & Adolescent Mental Health, British Psychological Society, and Lifetime Achievement award from the National Academy of Psychology.

**Kshama Rau** developed a passion for performing arts from her father and became an accomplished Odissi dancer and a dance teacher. After graduating in chemistry, she trained in Odissi at the Kalakshetra in Chennai and later received advanced training under Guru Kelucharan Mahapatra. She directs her dance school Nrithya Shilpa in Bengaluru. Kshama Rau is a member of the advisory committee of established by the Government of Karnataka to oversee the restoration of Shivarama Karanth's Balavana.

# Praise for *Growing Up Karanth*

'To have met Shivarama Karanth was to know one was in the presence of greatness. To learn about his astonishing range of interests, and to read his writings (even in translation), was to recognise that only Rabindranath Tagore ranked alongside him on the scale of his achievement. And yet, as someone who met Karanth and venerates him for his work, I have longed to know more about the human being as distinct from the Renaissance Man. My longings have now been satisfied by this wonderful book, written by Karanth's three children, each a distinguished professional. *Growing Up Karanth* is at once a biography of a remarkable couple (the sections on Leela Karanth are particularly moving) and a wider cultural history of modern South India. The book is rich in insight and anecdote, as well as unflinchingly honest, as in the descriptions of their mother's depression and of their father's bouts of anger.

'*Growing Up Karanth* is made more special still through its tender and empathetic foreword, written by that other jewel of modern Karnataka, Chiranjiv Singh.' —**Ramchandra Guha, historian**

'In *Growing Up Karanth*, Ullas Karanth, Malavika Kapur, and Kshama Rau tell the fascinating story of their father, Shivarama Karanth, a luminary of the 20th-century Kannada literary, artistic, scientific, and political worlds. A household name in Karnataka, Karanth's awe-inspiring list of achievements has remained shamefully neglected outside the state. This book will go a long way towards reviving his well-deserved reputation as an inspirational polymath of India.' —**Shashi Tharoor, writer and Member of Parliament**

'*Growing Up Karanth* is an affectionate, honest, and objective biography of Karnataka's first citizen of literature, by his highly accomplished children. It brings out vividly Sri Shivarama Karanth's multifarious personality—a naughty and curious child among children; a glittering savant among the cognoscenti; and a dynamic and energetic iconoclast standing tall, amidst the "wimpy" and "invertebrate" environment of our generation. Reading this unputdownable book brought back vivid memories of my own two-hour meeting with Shivarama Karanth at Kota in 1995. It is a must-read for every English-literate Indian.' —**N.R. Narayana Murthy, Founder Chairman, Infosys**

'Kota Shivaram Karanth was a creative genius who enriched the life and culture of his native Karnataka region while casting a light upon the wider world. His many contributions in the realms of art, dance, education and literature marked him as a major figure of modern India, while he championed [the] recognition of the Kannada language and the realization of a unified Karnataka. *Growing Up Karanth* offers a brilliant and touching portrait of the man and his times as seen through the eyes of his children. Their portrayals of Karanth's personality and his connections to the rich complexities of his social networks offer invaluable insights while sensitively invoking the rhythms of [the] rural society of his native South Kanara district.' —**Frank F. Conlon, Professor Emeritus of History and South Asian Studies, University of Washington, Seattle, USA**

'Here are personal reflections on the great Shivarama Karanth by his three children. *Chomana Dudi, Bettada Jeeva,* [and] *Marali Mannige* are a few of the masterpieces of Shivarama Karanth. The legacy of Shivarama Karanth has been woven together by the authors, and personal stories and anecdotes artistically put together. I really enjoyed reading the book and longed for those astonishing times to return.' —**C.N.R. Rao, former Director, The Indian Institute of Science**

'Memoir of the decade: A period piece of an era of great efflorescence including black and whites of the 1930s. An amazing, awe-inspiring, warts-and-all memoir by three siblings of famous parents. Kota Shivarama Karanth was at the centre of, and in some ways was the storm—and how! He did not find his own Boswell, but this trio has written a remarkable memoir of his times.' —**Mahesh Rangarajan, Professor of History and Environmental Studies, Ashoka University, Haryana**

'Even in what was an amazing era of great writers in Kannada literature, Shivarama Karanth was a giant. His novels are still read and loved. However, for us, the children of the Kannada playwright "Shriranga", he was also the "Photo-Mama", who clicked many excellent pictures of us. I had to read his *Marali Mannige* to know him as a novelist. And become a writer myself to know the great curiosity readers have about a writer's life. This book, co-authored by Karanth's three children, gives the readers glimpses of Karanth as a family man and as a father. —**Shashi Deshpande, writer**

'Writing about a man who has the personality of mythical proportions is perilous if not impossible. The instant work stands out for its hitherto unexplored faces ... well-written and highly captivating the book is a must-read for admirers of Sri. Karanth.' —**Jagadguru Sri Shivarathri Deshikendra Mahaswamigalu, Seer of Sutturu Matha, Karnataka**

'I am sure the book *Growing Up Karanth* will be accepted by readers with enthusiasm. I heartily congratulate the authors for their contribution and memories of Shivarama Karanth which hitherto were not in [the] public domain.' **—Justice N. Santosh Hegde, Supreme Court of India (Retired), former Lokayukta, Karnataka**


## Media Reviews

'*Growing Up Karanth* is a radiantly powerful and beguiling biography that gives an insight into the life and times of Kota Shivarama Karanth. It's a warm and revealing book, abounding in images so vivid that a reader enters into the time and terrain of his life like a participant.' **—Neelam Mansingh Chowdhry, *The Tribune***

'This is what makes *Growing Up Karanth* (Westland), a book of memoirs by his three children, a literary event of great importance ... a detailed cultural memoir bringing alive a world and period which saw the multi-pronged negotiation of a regional culture with modernity introduced by colonialism. Growing up Karanth was a uniquely personal experience for each of the writers. "No one else can claim that rare privilege" as they say. They are wrong. All readers can claim that privilege, by proxy.' **—Rajendra Chenni, *The Hindu***

'It takes us inside the life and minds of the Karanth family ... There are many types of biographies. The ones I like are exactly like *Growing Up Karanth*—written not as a worshipful hagiography but as gritty reality ... may readers will lose themselves in the book.' **—Shobha Narayan, *Hindustan Times***

'If the term "renaissance man" can apply to anyone, the Kannada polymath Kota Shivarama Karanth would qualify ... it is not merely a retelling of the life of Shivarama Karanth, but an insight into what it was to grow up with him as a father. A memorable insight into not just man Karanth was, but the family he was a part of.' **—Madhulika Liddle, *The New Indian Express***

'He [Karanth] dropped out of college, joined the freedom movement, and also remained at the forefront of the [Karnataka] unification movement. He was an atheist, rationalist, believed in scientific temper and achieved major innovations in Yakshagana. And, of course, created an extraordinary world of fiction. Reading the book is an uplifting experience.' **—Deepa Ganesh, *Mint Lounge***

'An unconventional biography of an extraordinary man, this work by Karanth's children is chock-full of anecdotes, insights, and intimate details. That said, the book is, at its core, an honest attempt to describe what it is like to be the children of a creative genius, a "rare privilege" as they put it.' —**Jagdish Angadi,** *Deccan Herald*

'It is the format of the biography which makes it special. The candour and openness with which each of them writes is something amazing. Overall, the book is with the time you spend on it to get introduced to one of the makers of modern India.' —**Meena Raghunathan,** *Millennial Matriarchs*

# GROWING UP
# KARANTH

K. ULLAS KARANTH, MALAVIKA KAPUR
AND KSHAMA RAU

First published by Westland Non-Fiction, an imprint of Westland Publications Private Limited, in 2021

Published by Westland Non-Fiction, an imprint of Westland Books, a division of Nasadiya Technologies Private Limited, in 2022

No. 269/2B, First Floor, 'Irai Arul', Vimalraj Street, Nethaji Nagar, Allappakkam Main Road, Maduravoyal, Chennai 600095

Westland, the Westland logo, Westland Non-Fiction and the Westland Non-Fiction logo are the trademarks of Nasadiya Technologies Private Limited, or its affiliates.



ISBN: 9789395767187

10 9 8 7 6 5 4 3 2 1



Typeset by SÜRYA, New Delhi

Printed at Nutech Print Services-India

*TO OUR PARENTS*

*SHIVARAMA KARANTH*

*and*

*LEELA KARANTH*

# Contents

# FOREWORD

Karanth, Kuvempu, Bendre—the trinity of modern Kannada literature; the pride of Kannadigas; three distinct personalities representing three distinct cultural regions of Karnataka: Kota Shivarama Karanth, coastal Karnataka; Kuppali Venkatappa Puttappa, Old Mysore; Dattatreya Ramachandra Bendre, northern Karnataka.

It was Shivarama Karanth who took the culture of Karnataka beyond the shores of India with his dance and music. After Rabindranath Tagore, no one had mastered as many art forms as Shivarama Karanth. Tagore was a major inspiration to Karanth. He had visited Shantiniketan as a young man. It was fitting, therefore, that years later Tagore's Visva-Bharati University awarded him its honorary doctorate, Desikottam. Tagore and Karanth were similar in many ways, both polymaths. The title of Karanth's autobiography in Kannada, *Hucchu Manasaina Hatthu Mukhagalu*, was rendered in English as *Ten Faces of a Crazy Mind*. It was translated by his friend and admirer, H.Y. Sharada Prasad. 'Ten faces' is an understatement, though.

I first met Shivarama Karanth in the early 1970s. It was at a meeting chaired by the chief minister of Karnataka, Devaraja Urs. Everyone present deferred to Karanth. With his leonine face and handsome figure, he dominated the gathering. Behind that formidable presence there was a lifetime of hard work and achievement. Genius alone, even an incandescent one like Karanth's, is not enough. After all, it was Thomas Edison who said, 'Genius

is one per cent inspiration and ninety nine per cent perspiration.'
Karanth worked hard all his life. His achievements are astonishing.
And that made his public persona forbidding. But to those who
knew him well, he was like a mighty tree alive with bird song in its
luxuriant canopy.

His children, Malavika Kapur, Ullas Karanth and Kshama Rau,
have narrated what it was like growing up being 'Karanth'. This book
is not a conventional biography of the great man; it is the children's
homage to a loving father, while also setting the record straight. They
do not flinch from reality and tell the truth; this is a trait inherited by
them from their parents. Their father's greatness is well-known. But
as they have recorded, their mother, Leela Karanth was great in her
own right. This book is a tribute as much to her as to him. Finally
Leela Karanth gets her due.

Chiranjiv Singh with Tata

Being married to Karanth was not easy for her. But her love and
generosity made light the difficulties of being married to a genius. In
this affectionate account Karanth is someone who, for all the freedom
he gave to his children, did not exactly believe in sparing the rod.

No one has written as much for children in Kannada as Karanth has. Here too the similarity with Tagore is remarkable. Tagore wrote Bengali primers for children; Karanth wrote them in Kannada. After I learnt to read Kannada, the first books that I read were the Amar Chitra Katha stories written by Shivarama Karanth. It is not generally known that the early Amar Chitra Kathas were written by Shivarama Karanth. The project was the brainchild of G.K. Anantharam, who headed IBH Publications in Bangalore. He asked Karanth to write the text, which he did, for the sake of children. Anantharam got the text illustrated. They were later translated into English and as is often the case, the English editor got the credit. The real credit belongs to Anantharam and Shivarama Karanth. The first book on Karnataka that I bought was titled *Picturesque South Kanara*, written by Shivarama Karanth. It had beautiful photographs taken by him.

The presence of genius can be intimidating. Kalpana, one of the top stars of Kannada cinema, who was the heroine of *Maleya Makkalu*, a film made by Karanth, said that she was 'overawed by Karantharu', while being directed by him. It showed. Critics found the performance of that fine actress stilted. Ullas has talked about the making of *Maleya Makkalu*. Karanth had to do things himself, had to experience them—even making a feature film.

To me, the author of Amar Chitra Kathas, the grandfatherly teller of tales, was always affectionate. When he came to Mysore or Bangalore, he would telephone me and say, 'I am here.' In Bangalore, 'here' was Janardhana Hotel where a ground floor room was kept for him. I would leave whatever I was doing and go to see him. Those meetings were unforgettable.

He never said no to any request made by me. When I requested that he should agree to get a documentary made on him by the department of information, he readily agreed, though earlier he had refused. He only laid down the condition that the documentary should be made by B.V. Karanth. When I requested him to agree to accept the 'Karnataka Rajyaprashashti', which celebrates the

unification of Karnataka—after he had refused all awards in protest
of the Emergency imposed by Indira Gandhi—he agreed, on the
condition that Sham. Ba. Joshi also be given the award. He agreed to
be a member of the Hampi Development Authority, and also agreed
to inaugurate the first World Kannada Conference at Mysore along
with Kuvempu at my request.

Karanth was generous in friendship. Ullas has written about his
friends and mentors. The role of these mentors and friends in his life
was important.

I remember him talking about K.K. Hebbar often. Hebbar was
my friend too. I invited both Karanth and Hebbar together to the
Administrative Training Institute, Mysore. I got them to plant a
neem tree (*Azadirachta indica*) and a peepal tree (*Ficus religiosa*) side
by side. In Karnataka, neem and peepal are married ritually. This
planting was to commemorate their friendship.

Kshama has written of how Karanth stopped the 'restoration' of
the great Ugra Narasimha statue at Hampi. I remember that. *The
Hindu* had carried a news item about the restoration. I was surprised
to read it. I called the director general of the Archaeological Survey
of India who was getting the restoration done. He, an old friend, was
convinced that what he was doing was right. I called Karanth and
told him about it. He arrived in Bangalore the next day, impatient to
go to Hampi.

We left for Hampi the next morning. It was a long journey and
the road was bad. He told me to take him straight to the site, without
taking rest. His energy at that age was astonishing.

What we saw there was appalling. Karanth was enraged. He
was so angry that he could barely speak. For a moment I was afraid
he would get a stroke. He was red in the face. I took him to the
government rest house. The next day we returned and he wrote to the
prime minister, Rajiv Gandhi. The statue was saved.

Malavika, Ullas and Kshama have revealed the softer side of
Karanth. Their narration complements his autobiography and
reminiscences. No account of Karanth's life will henceforth be

complete without reference to this memoir. Their memories of their mother, Leela Karanth, are the most significant part of this book. It is a moving account. As they say, '(She) made many sacrifices so that he could realise his dreams.'

This book is interesting also as a cultural study of the communities of South Kanara. I, for one, did not know that there was one kind of rice for the Bunts and one for the Brahmins. The Karanth marriage was an inter-caste Brahmin–Bunt marriage. Vignettes of characters from various communities like Leela Karanth's grandmother, Mallappe, and her version of the Ramayana, the family history of the Karanths of Kota and the description of their 'Kota Mahajagattu' make this an interesting cultural document, besides being the account of a culturally unique family.

Ullas has also written about his father's foray into politics and elections. When Karanth contested the parliamentary election from Karwar in 1989, I was the election observer. He filed his nomination papers and told me that he was leaving for America. He left Karwar, and his acolytes campaigned for him. That was the only time when I saw that all election rules were scrupulously followed. Those were Karanth's instructions. Like Ullas, I too felt sorry that Anant Nag, the brilliant actor, lost to a third candidate because of Karanth. The genius could also be naïf.

Karanth had a fine sense of humour, a dry kind of humour which is there in his novels. During the first World Kannada Conference, a few writers were discussing with Karanth about the glorious cultures of Karnataka. One writer offered to accompany Karanth to Shravanabelagola Hill to see the Digambara (naked) statue of Gommateshwara, a great figure with fine genitalia, a magnificent work of art. Karanth smiled and said, 'Why should I climb the hill to see what I see every day in the bathroom?'

The last phase of Karanth's life makes for sad reading. His amanuensis became his secretary, gatekeeper and controller. This is the stuff of many a work of fiction, except that in this case it happened. The slow disintegration of a strong personality was tragic.

The children's account of his last years leaves one reflecting on the vagaries of life.

Mrs Leela Karanth had said, 'This Karanth is not a real person. He is a gifted actor. His entire life is an enactment by that actor. No real individual could have lived life this way and accomplished so much in a single lifetime.' When the lights faded on the gifted actor, the outpouring of grief from the public was overwhelming. He belonged as much to them as to the family.

A lot has been written about Karanth's life and letters. But sufficient attention has not been paid to his linguistic experiments. One of the difficulties in doing technical writing in Indian languages is the limitation of technical vocabulary. How he overcame that when writing on science and technical subjects needs to be studied. The Karnataka government had set up committees to create technical vocabulary. These committees should have followed Karanth's lead. He was way ahead of his time. In this age of information technology and artificial intelligence, his scientific writings are more relevant than ever. Interest in science and technology is another quality Tagore and Karanth shared. Both tried to uplift their language and make it a vehicle for science and technical writing.

One hopes that Shivarama Karanth's contribution to the formation of the Kannada cultural identity and to the enrichment of Kannada language would be rediscovered. This biography by his three children would surely contribute to that.

**Chiranjiv Singh**

# WHY THIS BOOK?

All three of us are now in our seventies. Obviously, the question may arise why we are writing this book a quarter century after our father Shivarama Karanth's death. There are many reasons, some shared among the three of us, others unique to each one of us. Our individual narratives will perhaps make these reasons clearer.

All his children, following a tradition set by our deceased elder brother Harshanna (Harsha Karanth, 1938-61), always addressed our father as 'Tata' (pronounced Thatha, literally meaning 'grandfather'). In this intimate portrait, we will continue that practice. We have also labelled our mother, and a few others, with similar familiarity.

Busy as we were with our own careers, we had no plans to jointly write a book on Tata. We could not have written this book while he was still alive. Even after we came around to the idea of compiling his personalised biography, with much encouragement from Tata's friend and admirer Chiranjiv Singh, our intention was not to write an uncritical hagiography. Writing an honest book about Tata, Amma and our relationships with them turned into a far more complex task than we had imagined.

Our initial idea of collaborating with two professional writers did not pan out. The next plan was to assemble the book, with ourselves as editors, by collating narratives by many people who knew Tata well. This approach also led to a dead end, because of difficulties in weaving a cohesive narrative from the patchy and varied accounts we could gather. Finally, as our own professional obligations became less intense, we managed to find the time to create this narrative.

The book, while being the product of our collective labour, has also been structured such that each of us had the space to reminisce individually. So, while the first and second chapters are jointly written, they set the stage for the individual narratives that follow. (Malavika in chapters 3 and 4, Ullas in chapters 5, 6 and 7 and Kshama in chapters 8 and 9.) This, we believe, has ensured that all of us can narrate our individual experiences while also being part of the collective one.

In large part, this book is our tribute to Tata and Amma, celebrating the gifts they gave us while we were 'growing up Karanth'. Chief among these gifts was the motivation to make a career out of whatever we felt passionately about and to live honestly, holding our heads high. However, sticking to these credos while we wrote this book has not been easy. We can only say we have tried hard.

There are many memories here in this book that we truly cherish. However, we also had to honestly portray how the fairy tale marriage of our parents turned sour after a quarter century; how Amma's robust personality crumbled under debilitating mental and physical illnesses, inflicting intense loneliness and mental agony on Tata; how in the final decade of his life Tata unfairly distanced so many individuals who loved him dearly and had supported him tirelessly; how Tata's loneliness and poor judgement were exploited by a self-serving companion. And in the end how Tata, the vigorous and refined renaissance man, was turned into a sad old man engulfed by his singular obsession.

With all these emotional ups and downs, writing this book has been an exhilarating as well as cathartic experience for us. We hope our readers will appreciate our effort and forgive any inadvertent errors and omissions.

*Ullas Karanth*
*Malavika Kapur*
*Kshama Rau*

# 1

# SHIVARAMA KARANTH
## *A GENIUS IN THE MAKING*

*Ullas Karanth, Malavika Kapur, Kshama Rau*

Kota Shivarama Karanth: 'Tata' in our memories

## *Our 'Tata'*

Our father, Kota Shivarama Karanth (1902-97), was a protean genius who dominated the Kannada cultural scene for the better part of the twentieth century. His achievements in the varied domains that he so passionately engaged with are truly mind-boggling. Perhaps no other contemporaneous intellectual in India can match the way he straddled the diverse worlds of art, letters, popular science and social activism. His world was not a carefully cultivated academic intellectual one, conveniently insulated from the messy, tumultuous real world. Unlike most other Kannada writers, Karanth never held a salaried job in his life. He engaged in the rough and tumble of an activist's life when he was barely twenty, by dropping out of college to plunge into the freedom struggle.

Although Shivarama Karanth has been a household name in Karnataka for close to a century, his genius and accomplishments are not as well-known outside. Some are probably aware that he is famous for 'something', but they are not sure exactly what that 'thing' is.

As for Kannadigas, while they have become increasingly literate and prosperous, ironically, the readership of Kannada books and magazines is declining among them. They profess admiration for Shivarama Karanth, whose image they can recognise on the yellow and red banners lauding Kannada displayed all over Karnataka. However, they don't seem to appreciate the magnitude of his contributions to their own culture and society.

Kannadigas abroad do recognise Shivarama Karanth's name, but know little else about him. We hope that among the coming generations in this Kannadiga diaspora, there will be at least some who would dig a bit deeper below the surface of their 'Indian' identity. An account of the life and times of Karanth may offer Kannadigas abroad a window for such explorations of their roots. We also hope our narrative around the personal struggles and accomplishments of a man who contributed so much to the formation of the Kannada identity would be of value to all those who seek to understand the making of modern India in the twentieth century.

As his children, collectively and singly, the three of us had proximate access to Shivarama Karanth for over six decades. We hope an honest account of his personal life covering this period would also be a useful contribution to the social history of Kannadigas and their land.

For all these reasons, we have made this effort to assemble our account.

Tata's great accomplishments were not stand-alone efforts. He was supported unflinchingly, through his most difficult, and most creative years, by our Amma (Leela Karanth [1919-86]). We have tried to do justice to her contributions in this account.

Tata and Amma

While growing up, Tata was lucky to be mentored by some remarkable persons senior to him. His subsequent accomplishments were also enabled by the staunch support he received from some of his peers and friends. There were also many younger admirers who selflessly served him, with very little expectation in return. Finally, there were exceptional individuals employed by him, without whom his life would have been much harder.

The critical role of all these people—who turned Karanth the 'individual' into Karanth the 'institution'—remains hidden from most of his fans and readers. We believe their contributions to the ultimate flowering of Tata's genius should be put on the public record. We also share with the readers some facets of his personal life and struggles, as a husband, a father and a family man.

The first problem we faced when we took up this narrative was that a lot has already been written about Tata. He had written three autobiographies, the first version of *Huchchu Manasina Hatthu Mukhagalu* (Ten Faces of a Whimsical Mind),[1][*] *Smrithi Pataladinda* (Memories on the Screen),[2] written during the years 1977-79, and finally, *Alidulida Nenapugalu* (Fragments of My Memory) in 1995.[3] Furthermore, numerous other scholars, journalists and admirers had written or compiled excellent articles and books about Tata and his work.[4] Therefore, we had to seriously ponder how we could add any value to this rich corpus of writings.

What does this book contain? Every individual's life history unfolds in a specific historical and social context. In the first two chapters, we have tried to provide such contexts in the case of both Tata and Amma.

We have briefly described the social and family backgrounds of both our parents, their relationship and key turning points in their lives that preceded our births (Malavika in 1940, Ullas in 1948 and Kshama in 1950) in the first two chapters. We hope this provides our readers with the background to unpack our personal narratives in chapters 3 to 9. The three of us join hands again as co-authors in the final chapter.

In all these chapters, we have tapped into our distinct memories of the years we spent with our parents. We do not claim to be unbiased biographers, emotionally detached from our subjects. For good or bad, bits of our own life stories and feelings are woven into the fabric of this book.

The three of us offer very different perspectives on the events we

---

1    See B-1 in Annotated Bibliography for more details

*    While many of Tata's works have been translated into English, the English translations we have provided in brackets thorughout the book are not necessarily the names of the translated works. They are translations more for the benefit of the reader regarding the themes of his works.

2    See B-2 in Annotated Bibliography for more details

3    See B-3 in Annotated Bibliography for more details

4    B-4 to B-11 in Annotated Bibliography provide a good sample

describe. This is but natural because the three of us are very different personalities. We grew up in somewhat different circumstances. Each of us was treated differently by our parents. We hope this heterogeneity among perspectives enriches rather than detracts from the stories we tell.

Shivarama Karanth, the man, had many positive qualities as well as a few negative ones. Many of these are known only to a few individuals who witnessed the events we describe. We had ringside seats as witnesses to events in this story. Sometimes we were also participants.

No one else can perhaps narrate this story like we can.

## Tata and his background

The world in which Tata grew up is brilliantly captured in some of his well-known novels like *Marali Mannige* (Return to the Homeland),[5] perhaps nowhere better than in his fictionalised vignettes on prominent personalities of Kota, titled *Halliya Hatthu Samastharu* (Ten Respectable Persons in the Village).[6] Caricaturing caste characteristics, as Tata does superbly in this classic, we believe is a more readable alternative to structured social anthropology. We have borrowed this technique in trying to capture the milieu of our narrative.

The Kota Brahmana, the Brahmin subsect into which Tata was born, is one of our roots too. Kota Brahmins use a dozen or so surnames, such as Karantha, Mayya, Adiga, Holla, Hande, etc. The surname 'Karantha' is derived from the word 'Karyavantha' (an entrepreneur, or one who gets things done).

Among the Brahminical intellectual traditions, Kota Brahmins follow the Advaita philosophy expounded by Shankaracharya in the eighth century CE. However, unlike other Advaita sects who worship the god Shiva, the Kota Brahmins' primary deity is

---

5    See B-12 in Annotated Bibliography for more details
6    See B-13 in Annotated Bibliography for more details

Narasimha, the half-lion avatara of Vishnu. Going a step further, Kota Brahmins have boldly proclaimed themselves as the highest-ranking among all Brahmin sects in the whole world—so high, in fact, that they do not accept any human being, including Shankaracharya, as their Guru. Consequently, Kota Brahminical tradition forbids the falling at the feet of any human Guru. Instead, they claim Narasimha as their sole Guru. To match their real estate with this claim of exalted spiritual status, they have formally titled a cluster of fourteen villages around Kota as 'Kota Mahajagattu' (the great universe of Kota).

The word 'Kota', when correctly pronounced by the local cognoscenti, phonetically sounds like 'Qwata'. In the Kundapura dialect of Kannada spoken by them, the equivalent of the American 'Hi' is a cheerful 'Hoy' delivered at a high-decibel level across long distances.

Although it matters little in the larger scheme of things, we must confess that we are disappointed that recent generations have given up on the Kota Brahmins' unique traditional claims of grandeur. Kota Brahmins now readily fall at the feet of sundry human Gurus, thus abdicating their unique privilege of reporting directly to God without any intermediaries.

As narrated in his autobiographies, Tata was first educated in Kota. He and his siblings had to shed all their clothes and bathe outside the house to ritually cleanse themselves after returning home from the company of 'lower caste' students at the village school. Later, he went on to study in the town of Kundapur, where his father had established a 'bidaara' (boarding camp) to enable his sons to study in the only high school in that part of the district.

Swept up by tides of new revolutionary ideas blowing across the country, soon the rebel in Tata rejected most Brahminical orthodoxies, shedding his 'janiwara' (sacred thread) in his late teens. After years of a soul-searing search for God, wandering across the physical and intellectual terrains earlier traversed by Buddha, Ramakrishna Paramahamsa and the Hindu reformists from Bengal, Tata discarded all these paths. He became a rationalist, and even a vocal atheist, who acerbically lampooned Brahminical orthodoxy in his early literary works like *Gnana* (Deep Knowledge) and *Devadootharu* (God's Messengers).[7]

When Tata was a student in the Government College at Mangalore in 1922, Kannappa, who was his teacher, one day found him in a pensive mood. When asked the reason, Tata had said he did not find college education useful to his life's journey. The very next day, Tata quit college and joined India's freedom movement that had just been reinvigorated by the charismatic messiah, Mohandas Karamchand Gandhi.

Tata became an ardent follower of Mahatma Gandhi, struggling tirelessly to advance causes such as the promotion of khadi and cottage industries, abolition of untouchability, eradication of traditional caste-based concubinage and the promotion of adult literacy.

Tata's actions caused much unhappiness within his extremely orthodox family and community. Even Tata's father, Shesha Karanth, a remarkably audacious man in his own right, shed tears of disappointment over the life choices Tata was making. Shesha Karanth's closest friend, one Narayana Mayya, had tried to placate him saying although the renegade Shivarama had abandoned Brahminism, he had seven other fine sons to be torch-bearers of tradition. Shesha Karanth had retorted that Mayya had no idea of the true worth of his fourth son Shivarama, 'who is weightier than all the others combined'.[8]

## The Karanths of Kota[9]

The roughly reconstructed genealogy of the Karanth family begins with a Kota Vasudeva Karantha, about whom we know little else.

---

7    See B-14 and B-15 in Annotated Bibliography for more details

8    See B-16 in Annotated Bibliography for more details

9    See B-16 in Annotated Bibliography for more details relating to this section

His son Parameshwara Karantha was, however, a wealthy landlord. Unfortunately, Parameshwara lost his entire fortune in trying to transform copper into gold through ancient Hindu alchemy. Parameshwara Karantha thereafter promptly disappeared, abandoning his wife and children to their fate. Tata's father, Shesha Karanth (1868-1940), was the only son of that doomed alchemist. This is a tale that Tata's younger sister Yamuna Rao had heard during her childhood, and shared with Malavika.

Whatever the truth of this tale is, it is clear Kota Shesha Karanth began from a humble background. He worked as a clerical assistant to the Hande family, then considered the wealthiest among the Brahmins of Kota. Through sheer hard work and enterprise, Shesha Karanth later prospered, became a landlord, a merchant and a well-known philanthropist. Shesha Karanth's bronze bust now adorns the forecourt of the school he founded in Giliyaru near Kota, which is popularly known as 'Giliyaru Shaale' in preference to its incredibly longwinded formal name: Shambhavi Vidyadayinee Hiriya Prathamika Shaale.

Because of his fairness and gravitas, people often came to Shesha Karanth to resolve disputes among themselves. Our cousin, Someshwar Shyam Sunder (1931-2021), an eminent forester and Yamuna Rao's son, recounts a poignant incident that he witnessed as a little boy. Two groups of angry men had violently clashed over some property dispute. They had come to Shesha Karanth for arbitration, on a pitch-dark night. There were only dim lanterns to cast any light. At the centre was a profusely bleeding young man, whose arm had been nearly severed with a machete. How our grandfather took control of the situation, diffused their anger, ensured the injured man was rushed to the hospital and patiently resolved the dispute had remained indelible in Shyam Sunder's memory.

Tata's mother, Mahalakshmi from Parampalli, was a tough, traditional lady. She gave birth to eleven children, of whom ten survived. Tata had two sisters and seven brothers. Shesha Karanth and Mahalakshmi also adopted and raised two more girls, who were daughters of a close friend who died suddenly. According to our uncle, K.L. Karanth, a son of one of these ladies raised by our grandparents was H.V. Hande, a well-known medical doctor in Madras, who later rose to political prominence as a leader and minister in the AIADMK government that ruled Tamil Nadu in the 1980s.

How our grandmother Mahalakshmi Karanth managed such a large 'menagerie' of mischievous boys of varying ages, while also doing housework and farm work, is quite a story. When our Amma had asked her this, she learned that her mother-in-law's trick was to mix a tiny bit of opioid into the meals of the most recalcitrant among the boys to prevent things from getting out of hand!

Among his siblings, Tata greatly respected his eldest brother Ramakrishna Karanth (K.R. Karanth, 1894-1980) who was a tall leader in the Congress Party during the freedom struggle. In the pre-independence era of limited-franchise elections, K.R. Karanth was elected twice to the legislature of the Madras Presidency. He served first as a political secretary to the chief minister, C. Rajagopalachari (Rajaji), and later as revenue minister in the government headed by T. Prakasham. Later, K.R. Karanth and Prakasham resigned, protesting the rising corruption in the Congress Party and joined the Praja Socialist Party (PSP) formed by Acharya Kripalani and other leaders.[10]

Tata was even closer to his second elder brother, Lakshminarayana Karanth (K.L Karanth, 1898-1994), a science teacher of repute, a great horticulturist and a generous philanthropist in Kundapur.[11] He too was an atheist like Tata, although the rest of his lifestyle was more conventional. He and Tata used to meet often to discuss science and rationalist philosophies.

---

10   See B-17 in Annotated Bibliography for more details
11   See B-18 in Annotated Bibliography for more details

Tata with elder brother Lakshminarayana (K.L.) Karanth, a rationalist like him. K.L. Karanth was an eminent teacher, horticulturist and philanthropist.

Tata's youngest brother, Parameshwara Karanth (K.P. Karanth, 1916-99), obtained his doctoral degree in pharmacology in Switzerland in 1948. K.P. Karanth made his fortune establishing a pharmaceutical company in Hyderabad. He retired to Bangalore in his later years. Tata was very fond of him, and sometimes even borrowed money from him. He was the most cosmopolitan and genial one among Tata's siblings. As Ullas puts it, 'He was the only uncle with whom I could chat with a drink in hand.'

Youngest brother Parameshwara (K.P.) Karanth with Tata. K.P. Karanth, with a doctorate from Switzerland, was a pioneer of pharmacological research in India.

Tata liked his other brothers too, but they did not share the same chemistry. Two brothers, his immediate elder, Vasudeva Karanth (K.V. Karanth; 1900-88), and the immediate younger, Shankaranarayana Karanth (K.S. Karanth; 1905-79), were men steeped in orthodoxy. The former was an eminent engineer who headed the electricity department of the Madras Presidency. The latter was a brilliant but acid-tongued lawyer in Mangalore, who was professionally not very successful. These two brothers spent only brief moments with Tata when they visited our home in Puttur. However, they chatted at length with Amma, sharing their joys and sorrows. Although their empathy with Amma was genuine, neither man ever ate or drank anything in our 'ritually polluted' home. Tata did occasionally help his other two younger brothers, Narasimha (1907-61) and Shivayya (1912-87), but did not interact much with them.

Tata was fond of his two younger sisters, Shridevi (1910-91) and Yamuna (1914-2007). He also liked their respective spouses, Sadashiva Rao (1903-96) and Venkata Rao (1907-91). The former was a leading lawyer in Puttur. He devoted decades of his life in rendering selfless service to orphaned children. Venkata Rao, one of Mangalore's leading lawyers, practised the prescriptions of the Bhagavad Gita. He truly was 'a man who did not have a mean bone in his body'.

Venkata Rao, Yamuna and Amma developed a close bond because of their interest in Hindu philosophy, and later, their shared devotion to Sathya Sai Baba of Puttaparthi.

## Amma and her family

By caste, Amma was a Bunt (pronounced Banta, meaning a warrior faithful to a king). Bunts served as generals as well as tax-collecting landlords under various feudal kingdoms that ruled over Kanara and Malenad. Here we use the term 'Kanara'—a British corruption of the word 'Kannada'—to specify a tract of land that now lies administratively splintered among the districts of Uttara Kannada,

Udupi and Dakshina Kannada in Karnataka, as well as the area north of the Chandragiri river in the present-day Kasaragod district of Kerala. Eventually, these warriors became the dominant landlord caste in South Kanara (Dakshina Kannada). Along the Kanara coast, Bunts also flourished as international traders operating from the two big ports of Mangalore and Barakuru (the mercantile surname Shetty is common among them). We cite from a richly detailed history of Bunts written by historian B. Surendra Rao.[12] (Surendra, who died in 2019, was a classmate of Ullas, and was a product of Puttur Board High School like all three of us.)

Bunts are a matriarchal community (like the two other numerically dominant castes of Kanara, the Billava and the Mogaveera). Under their traditional Aliya Santhana inheritance system, the property is passed on from the mother to her daughters, with male members of the family managing these lands rather than owning them. The wealthier landlord families among Bunts are organised into matriarchal clans called 'Guthu'. Bunts in the southern taluks of Kanara speak Tulu at home, whereas Bunts to the north of the Seethanadi river speak the Kundapura dialect of Kannada.

Amma was a Tulu speaker, born Leela Alva in Bombay on 21 September 1919. Her father was Kamu Alva (1887-1937), and her mother Kamala Alva. Following the matriarchal tradition, Amma traced her lineage to Kadenja Guthu, a landlord clan whose territory lay adjacent to Mangalore, across the Nethtravathi river. Our grandmother Kamala's maternal grand-uncle (Yajamana or headman of the Guthu) was Thyampanna Bhandari. He was a traditional 'bone-setter' (orthopedic 'fixer') who had invented, and held, the patent for the famed 'Kadenja Beneda Yenne' (a herbal oil remedy for pains and aches).

Amma told us a story she had heard from her mother about how the old bone-setter had fixed the dislocated arm of a patient quickly

---

12   See B-19 in Annotated Bibliography for more details

and skilfully, while being totally oblivious to the patient's agonised screams: it helped that Thyampanna Bhandari was stone deaf.

Amma's father Kamu Alva was from the Pavoor Guthu clan, but was not from its wealthy branch. His mother Akkamma (1862-1959) had been married twice. Widow remarriage was practised among Bunts long before the Hindu reformers struggled to introduce it among the self-proclaimed higher castes.

The three of us never saw our grandparents. However, Akkamma, who everyone addressed as 'Mallappe' (the great mother), was a part of our growing up during the years 1958-59.

Mallappe's first husband was a man named Poonja. They had a son named Mundappa Poonja. After her first husband died, Mallappe was married off to a Thyampanna Alva. She had two sons from this marriage. Our grandfather Kamu Thyampanna Alva (K.T. Alva) was born in 1887, followed by Gopala Alva born in 1890.

When Kamu Alva failed a school examination in 1902, feeling humiliated, he 'ran away to Bombay'. That is how people described the quiet departure of hundreds of fortune seekers from Kanara to Bombay as the twentieth century was dawning. Through sheer hard work and enterprise, Kamu Alva rose to become a prominent businessman. He partnered with a man, who we will call R, to establish a medical equipment trading company.

Alva's meteoric rise in Bombay can be gauged from the fact that he travelled to Germany by steamship, after the First World War, to import medical equipment. It is said that Kamu Alva was the first person in the Bunt community to travel abroad to the West.

When 300 Bunt men, all pioneers among the tough migrants, met in 1920 to form the Bunts Association of Bombay, Kamu Alva was elected as its treasurer.[13] He was clearly a leader among the Bunts of Kanara who had migrated to Bombay. Since those days Bunts have thrived in what is now Mumbai and became a part of the social fabric of the great city. They are now prominent as hoteliers,

---

13   See B-19 in Annotated Bibliography for more details

industrialists, film stars, sportspersons, politicians and even as dons of the underworld.

As he prospered in Bombay, Kamu Alva was joined by his mother Akkamma and brother Gopala Alva. In 1917, Kamu Alva got married to Kamala from Kadenja Guthu. She bore him five daughters. Leela, our Amma, was the second among them, with Savithri (1918-2005) being the eldest. They were followed by three younger sisters, Rathna, Ahalya (1927-86) and Sarojini.

After he prospered, Alva lived in a fancy bungalow in the Pali Hill area of Bombay. Amma had mentioned to Ullas about watching waves roll off the beaches of Chowpatty from her home, perhaps some time earlier. Amma could speak only her mother tongue Tulu and Marathi. She learned Kannada later, after moving to Mangalore at age eleven.

As stories go, Kamu Alva had given his power of attorney to his business partner to manage the company in his absence. The rumour is that the partner misused that document to take control of the company.

This is the story we heard: With her husband away in Germany, our grandmother Kamala Alva had to defend herself from threats made by Alva's partner to take possession of their house. Apparently, while her children slept upstairs at night, Kamala kept vigil near the front door holding a machete, ready to fend off the expected assailants.

Kamala Alva died in 1927, and our grandfather married Pushpavathi Shetty in 1928. By this time his brother Gopala Alva also appears to have lost much money betting on horse races. As his relationship with his business partner soured, in 1930, Kamu Alva had to retire from the company he founded, and move back to Mangalore. He was rumored have brought a large sum of cash as his share.

In 1931, Pushpavathi bore him his only son, Ramakrishna Alva (1931-85). We recall Amma saying how fond she was of her stepbrother. Ullas saw them together only once, in the late 1970s, when Ramakrishna Alva visited Amma in Saligrama—both were teary-eyed and hugged each other with joy.

In Mangalore, Kamu Alva settled down in the Bijai locality, on a large plot of land adjacent to the place where the government bus stand is now located. Apparently he lived a good life, maintaining a large, beautiful garden. His bungalow complex had three buildings, including one in which the servants and gardeners lived. He was wealthy enough to hobnob with the social elite of Mangalore. He became a good friend of the British district collector, E.M. Gowan, because of their shared passion for gardening. Attavara Balakrishna Shetty (1883-1960), a prominent Congress leader, who later became a minister in the Madras government, was also a good friend of Kamu Alva's.

However, Kamu Alva's second wife Pushpavathi appears to have been a cruel and manipulative woman. She ill-treated Amma and her four sisters. Kamu Alva too appears to have been an undiagnosed manic-depressive. He took to drinking and his health rapidly declined. Unable to bear the pain from the liver disease that afflicted him, Kamu Alva committed suicide by consuming poison on 1 April 1937.

## Mentors of the Renaissance Man

There is no doubt Tata was a genius, with a questioning mind and a rebellious strand in his DNA. But not all such talented men turn into bold thinkers who can walk away from faith and traditions as he did. Tata was born in an ultra-orthodox, inward-looking Brahmin sect. What made him unshackle himself from the chains of tradition? Clearly, the massive social changes that swept India after the colonial occupation by the British. But there were more proximate local factors too.

Tata has written in detail about the towering personalities who influenced him in his early years.[14] Other accounts mention his different mentors.[15] We present our brief narrative here based on

---

14   See B-1, B-2 and B-3 in Annotated Bibliography for more details
15   See B-4 to B-9 in Annotated Bibliography for more details

these accounts as well as conversations over the years with our parents and family members.

We believe Tata's young mind was shaped by his early exposure to the most literate and socially progressive community around him in Kanara. These people were the Chitrapur Saraswat Brahmins, who had migrated from Goa to Kanara to escape persecution and proselytisation by the Muslim and Portuguese rulers in earlier centuries.[16]

The Saraswats of Kanara were leaders of the social reform movements that strove to remove untouchability, other caste-based discriminations and promote widow remarriage, from the middle of the nineteenth century. Saraswat pioneers of grassroots social reforms included towering personalities like Kudmul Ranga Rao (1859-1928) who toiled lifelong to educate and uplift 'untouchable' castes by establishing his Depressed Classes Mission. He was also involved with the Brahmo Samaj Hindu reform movement in Mangalore. Even Mahatma Gandhi stood in awe of Ranga Rao's efforts at social reform, which had preceded his own efforts.[17]

Gulvadi Venkata Rao (1844-1913) pioneered the genre of modern Kannada (Hosa Kannada) novels. His path-breaking novel, *Indira Bai*, is about the plight of a child widow. Written in 1899, it advocated the emancipation of women. It also set the literary framework for the emerging modern Kannada literature. Gulvadi's reformist framework became the template for Tata's novels later.[18]

By the late nineteenth century, many Saraswats had risen to high levels in the service of the British colonial administration. Tata has spoken to Ullas particularly about Vombatkere Pandrang Row (1881-1946), who had grown up in poverty and studied under street lamps as a school student in Kundapur. Because of

16    See B-20 in Annotated Bibliography for more details
17    See B-10 and B-20 in Annotated Bibliography for more details
18    See B-4 in Annotated Bibliography for more details

his academic brilliance, Vombatkere travelled to England on a scholarship in 1901. He studied law at Cambridge University, qualified as a barrister, and was recruited into the Imperial Civil Service (ICS) in 1904. Vombatkere was the first Kannadiga to achieve that distinction. Ironically, upon returning home, he was compelled by elders to undergo rituals to 'purify' himself—for having violated the Brahminical prohibition against crossing the seas. Following Vombatkere, several other Saraswats, like Benegal Narasing Rau and Benegal Rama Rau, also rose to top levels in the colonial administration.[19]

At the same time, standing up politically in revolt against the same British colonial rulers was another Saraswat giant: Karnad Sadashiva Rao (1881-1944), one of the earliest and tallest leaders of the Congress Party led by Mahatma Gandhi. Karnad, one of the wealthiest landlords in South Kanara at that time, ultimately exhausted his entire personal fortune to build the Congress Party in Kanara. His social contributions and philanthropy were on an incredible scale: he personally funded the sheltering and feeding of thousands of people who were devastated by the floods that swept Kanara in 1923.

Karnad Sadashiva Rao was a significant mentor to Tata.[20] For all his generous service to society, Karnad died in penury after some Congress leaders he had nurtured conspired to suppress him politically. In Tata's great novel, *Audaryada Urulalli* (In the Noose of One's Own Generosity), we can discern Karnad in its tragic hero, Dayananda Rao.[21]

---

19   See B-20 in Annotated Bibliography for more details
20   See B-1 and B-2 in Annotated Bibliography for more details
21   See B-20 in Annotated Bibliography for more details

Freedom fighter and congress leader Karnad Sadashiva Rao,
a mentor to Tata, belonged to the Chitrapur Saraswat Brahmin
Community of Kanara, whose modernist and reformist influences
helped to shape Tata's attitudes and values early in his career.

While Tata was an upcoming writer and journalist, he stayed in Mangalore with Ramananda Rao Padukone (1886-1993), a chemistry teacher with varied cultural interests. At that time, Tata was trying to learn Hindustani classical music from an alcoholic genius named Sonam Singh, locally known as Lakdi Buwa because he earned his bread by working in a firewood depot.[22] Another family with whom Tata stayed was that of the English teacher Mundkur Ekambara Rao. In his autobiography, Tata refers to Mundkur as his 'Annadata'.[23]

During the 1920s Tata had tried hard to practice what Mahatma Gandhi preached. He met with failure at every corner: trying to sell handspun khadi to villagers who did not want it, trying to convince labourers that the drink they enjoyed at the end of the day was an evil to be shunned, and preaching eternal celibacy to girls in communities that traditionally turned them into consorts of rich men. Tata was

---

22   See B-1, B-2 and B-22 in Annotated Bibliography for more details
23   See B-1 to B-3 in Annotated Bibliography for more details

turning into a rationalist, atheist and a modernist. He appreciated the benefits that science, technology and medicine had gifted to society. He found Gandhi's anti-economic growth arguments, sex-denying prudery and god-fearing piety largely irrelevant to improving the lives of Indian citizens.

Tata's focus shifted towards social work by the 1930s, after his disenchantment with Mahatma Gandhi's economic and social ideologies. At this crucial juncture, Molahalli Shiva Rao (1881-1967), a prominent lawyer of Puttur became his mentor.[24] Under Molahalli's guidance, Tata worked to promote the upliftment of scheduled castes, community hygiene and rural literacy. Molahalli was also a pioneer of the cooperative society-based model of economic development. The district agricultural cooperative society and the bank he founded in South Kanara preceded Gujarat's far more famous AMUL venture by several decades. Molahalli's charisma enticed Tata, the eternal wanderer, to settle down in Puttur in 1930. With his backing, Tata established Balavana, which became the crucible for his innovative social and creative experiments in the next four decades.[25] Balavana was the place where we were all born and grew up.

Upon examining the influence of all these key mentors in his formative years, it appears to us that Shivarama Karanth's public persona was largely shaped by the refined sensibilities of the Kanara Saraswat community, rather than by his own more earthy Kota Brahmin traditions.

---

24  See B-1 to B-14 in Annotated Bibliography for more details
25  See B-1 to B-3 in Annotated Bibliography for more details

2

# THE 'AMMA' OF BALAVANA

*Malavika Kapur, Kshama Rau and Ullas Karanth*

### The sparkle of Amma

In this chapter, we focus on Amma and how her early relationship with Tata developed. Since much of this happened before we were born, we had to rely on what we heard from Amma as well as on published and unpublished accounts from friends and family.

In the text that follows, we have often borrowed heavily from the original accounts in Kannada by Tata[26] and others[27] as well as recalled information gleaned in conversations with friends and family members, most of whom are no more.

Amma was the second among Kamu Alva's five daughters. She was very intelligent and bold. Her father had told her he would send her abroad to study law and make her a barrister. However, her life took a strange turn. She lost her mother Kamala when she was just eight, and Kamu Alva got married again a year later. The little girls were looked after by their paternal grandmother, Akkamma. There was no peace at home because their stepmother Pushpavathi ill-treated the girls. Amma fought for the sake of her sisters, yet made

---

26    See B-1 and B-2 in Annotated Bibliography for more details
27    See B-23 to B-26 in Annotated Bibliography for more details

no demands for herself from her father. As her father's relationship with his partner R crumbled, Alva moved back to Mangalore in 1930, reportedly with a substantial amount of cash as his share.

After Kamu Alva returned to Mangalore, Amma and her sisters joined the Besant Girls School there. This was a fortunate turn of events for her. Many of the girls in that school were from educated and cultured families. Annie Besant and the theosophists were making valiant attempts to educate people about India's ancient culture and philosophy and this school had been set up to further their cause. They were also nurturing the freedom movement, clamouring for independence from colonial rule. There was a new awakening of sorts. Amma's fellow students were from such progressive and nationalistic families.

Although Amma did not know Kannada, having studied in Marathi medium in Bombay, she learnt it in no time. She excelled in her studies, as well as in dance and music. At that time Tata was conducting various cultural activities in Besant School. He was teaching dance and theatre to the girl students innovatively. Once he created a Japanese garden on the stage, and had students perform, wearing kimonos and holding paper fans. At another time, he recreated the Egyptian civilisation thematically. Amma was among his brightest and most talented students. Meanwhile, in Puttur, a small town fifty kilometres away, Tata had settled down to establish his home, the experimental venture he called Balavana.

Around 1935, Rama Bai Mundkur, who was the warden of the school hostel, brought the students to Balavana on a school excursion. This was Amma's first visit to Balavana. Apparently, Rama Bai had pointed out the lively girl Leela Alva to Tata as being especially talented, suggesting he should think about getting married to her.[28]

### Narrative of Vrinda Padukone

Vrinda Padukone (née Mundkur, 1925-2013), her cousin Vasantha

---

28   See B-1 in Annotated Bibliography for more details

Sathyashankar (née Mundkur 1921-82) and Amma became lifelong friends. Vrinda Padukone has recalled memories of Amma,[29] which we cite below:

> Leela was an intelligent girl. Her grasp of any topic was very quick. She was a favourite of all our teachers. There was no student in the group who did not know her. Students from all the classes were her friends. Whether it was curricular or non-curricular activities, Leela's abilities were extraordinary. She was an inspiration to all of us, and even to our teachers. She did not worry about her own family problems. Thus, to the world, it appeared as if Leela never had any problem. Only those of us close to her knew about the real hardships in her life.
>
> It is impossible to overstate the charisma of Leela's ever-smiling, enthusiastic personal traits, in the face of all the problems she faced at home. She participated in all school events and competitions without bothering at all about their outcomes. Selfishness was totally absent in her persona.
>
> Initially, when she arrived in Mangalore from Mumbai, Leela did not know Kannada. However, very soon she attained proficiency in Kannada, not only to speak but also read and write superbly. She was admired by all the teachers. We had school-sponsored activities such as the Girl Guides group. We played games such as Lezim and the fire drill. I recall that Leela could instantly learn any physical movements involved in these new activities and would soon start helping other students who found these harder.
>
> Even after Leela got married to Karanth, for some time, she stayed in the Besant School Hostel with me, to continue her studies. That year-long stay nurtured a strong bond between us. I got an opportunity to know Leela from close quarters. Leela's mindset was very mature and measured. At that time, although we were of

---

29   See B-24 in Annotated Bibliography for more details

similar age, I was not as mature in my understanding of the world. I realise that now.

Leela never liked to hurt anyone's feelings. However, she would become angry when she came across any instance of injustice. For the sake of fairness, she would strongly argue to establish the truth, regardless of the age or status of the person she was confronting. She was a very spiritual girl as well. She had immense faith in God.

As students, we had all visited Karanth's Balavana on a school trip. When we came to know about Leela's wedding to Karanth we wondered how she could survive in that wilderness of Balavana.

After her marriage, we witnessed Leela living there with redoubled enthusiasm and happiness. Leela got the opportunity to be the life partner of Karanth, a versatile personality. I believe this was her fate. It is not an easy task to live as an artiste's wife. Being a talented artiste herself, Leela adjusted to embellish her husband's life, assessing his varied needs and interests, and supporting them fully. In this process, she entirely neglected her own interests and needs. Leela lent support like an expert gardener to her husband so that he could cultivate his arts.

## *Tata and Amma: The fairy-tale marriage*

Over the years Amma has spoken to us and to others about how she met Tata, fell in love with him, and married him. In his biographies, Tata has also described these events.[30] In this section, we have woven these varied accounts into a single coherent story. While translating from Kannada, we have retained Amma's own words as much as possible:

I had a kind of disinterest in material objects right from my childhood. I don't remember ever being attracted to possess

---

30  Some of these original Kannada narratives are mentioned in B-24 in the Annotated Bibliography

something special to eat or wear as children usually are. I was content with whatever my elders provided. (This was said in the context of the ill-treatment of the sisters by their stepmother.)

However, I felt sad when I saw my sisters crying when they did not get what they had sought. Such occasions were frequent after we sisters lost our mother. I did not want to bother my father by making one demand or the other. However, for the sake of my sisters, I would cajole him to fulfil their demands. I never hesitated to be their advocate. Poor things, unlike me, they were afraid of the elders. Therefore, I had to be the mediator to speak on their behalf. I had no occasion to feel sad or cry for anything. I was happy with whatever I possessed.

I had never dreamt that one day I too would be compelled to make a demand for myself from my father!

However, that moment did arrive in my life, without any notice! I had such a strong desire coursing through me. The feeling that 'I must possess this' took over me, almost choking me emotionally.

It was odd how all these events unfolded rapidly.

I was studying at Besant Girls' School at Mangalore. The teachers were also training us in various extracurricular activities. Some of us friends were in the dance and drama training class. Shivarama Karanth was our dance teacher! The appointed day for staging some play was approaching. We were rehearsing hard for the day.

That was not the first time I had seen Karanth. Many a time I had been the target of his short temper during our drama rehearsals. I had also argued back with him more than any other student in the class.

On this day he had called all the girls to help him in making the costumes and jewellery needed for the play. Lots of gold and silver foils, coloured crepe papers and beads were spread out before him. With his nimble fingers literally dancing, Karanth wielded the scissors to cut out papers and foil, sticking them to create crowns, waistbands, armbands and such other costumes. He was so fast and so deft! I was mesmerised by those artistic hands. In the past, I had argued as well as chatted with him happily, along with my friends, without feeling such an emotion.

But this was a very decisive, strange moment in my life. Until then I did not know what I really wanted to possess in my life ... On that day, at that moment, I felt I had to possess those magical hands, forever. A strong desire filled my heart to make those hands exclusively mine. Those magical hands began to haunt me day and night after that moment.

Being a girl, the only way I could possess them was to marry the man.

Traditionally, a girl's mother is the conduit to carry a daughter's desires to her father. I wasn't that fortunate: I had already lost my mother. How I wished my mother were alive! After brooding over my dilemma for two days, I could see no other option than boldly opening my heart to my father.

At that moment, I remembered my father's promise to me, made years ago, after a curious incident in Bombay. One evening, I had been sitting on the balcony of our bungalow with my feet dangling over the edge. I was rather inattentively gazing at the sky or looking at the crowd on the street below. Involuntarily, I was also swinging my legs ...

A stranger walking on the street below had looked up and loudly and sarcastically commented: this girl will bring 'real fame' to her father.

My father, who was downstairs, heard those nasty comments. He shouted at me to come down. I came down, not even knowing what had upset him so much. My father then reprimanded me thus: 'Girls from respectable families should not swing their legs sitting outside like you have been doing. My dear child, I am aware that you didn't do this consciously. However, please don't do this again. Please don't do anything that would bring me shame. If you want anything at all in life, ever, please directly ask me for it. Even though your mother is no more, please do not hesitate to come to me. I will try to fulfil whatever your wish is.' That was my father's promise to me, made with much love.

After two days of dithering, I went to my father. I reminded my father that he had promised to give me whatever I wanted. Yet I had never made any demands, so far. I said, 'Now I am making one: I want to marry "Master".' (That is how all of us girls addressed Karanth.)

My father was shocked. 'How is it possible? Forget it,' he said. But I argued back and would simply not yield. Finally, he said, 'Alright, I will agree. You please invite him home to talk.'

I invited the 'Master' to come home, and showed him the beautiful garden my father had made. I then sprang it on him: 'I want to marry you!' He replied, 'Do you know what you are talking about? This is a serious matter. Think about it.' I told him, 'I have thought about it a lot, and this is what I want.' He said, 'Life with me can be very difficult for you.' He soon realised that I was very sure of my decision. Finally, he said, 'If that is what you want, I will say yes.'

In his autobiography,[31] Tata has also narrated those events:

She (Leela) had invited me to come to her home to see the famed garden her father had established. While I was there, strangely and abruptly she said she would marry me! I found it hard to immediately respond to such a question, one I had not even

---

31 See B-1 in Annotated Bibliography for more details

imagined she would so boldly ask, even if she had thought about it earlier. I responded cautiously: 'Have you thought deeply about this? There are issues such as my temperament, financial status, and the responsibilities that you will be taking on. You should not talk in this manner without forethought.' She told me she did not want to hear this advice from me. All she wanted to know was whether I would agree to her proposal. I told her while I did not disagree, we had to think more deeply. With that said, we entered the house to meet her father. Apparently, three days earlier she had already opened her heart to him. He had his own anxieties. He told me his income was also declining which was a factor to be considered, and then there was the issue of an inter-caste marriage. He advised me to think hard about all these issues. The same evening, I took Leela for a long walk, patiently explaining the challenges we would face if we went ahead. But her mind was firmly made up.

Tata and Amma got married in a simple civil ceremony at the registrar's office in Mangalore on 6 May 1936. The wedding was attended by only a few close friends. It was the full moon day, celebrated as Buddha Poornima. Tata laconically commented later that on that day he too became a 'Prabuddha' (wise one).

Tata and Amma as a newly married couple

The young couple braved a major social storm their inter-caste marriage raised in Kanara. Yet, their austere life was also rich with much joy and adventure. While Tata assiduously cultivated the arts and literature, Amma was able to control his short temper and rash traits. Amma continues her story.

The beginning of our married life was full of hardships. I stayed on as a student for nearly a year trying to complete the eighth grade, and taking additional English lessons from my teacher Sambrani Mukunda Rao. I lived in the Besant School hostel. Other girls in the hostel were from affluent families. On the weekends, they would go shopping for things they desired. I felt no need to buy anything.

On weekends, Karanth would visit me in the hostel. I longed for his visits. Before leaving, he would ask me, 'Do you want some money?' He would then dip his large palm into his deep pockets trying to fish out some money to give me. He would find only a handful of coins and spread them out on my outstretched palm. I had to carefully cup my hands to ensure they would not roll off my palm. After he left, I would count the coins: they added up to very little money—usually less than half a rupee. I never felt bad about how little money Karanth had. In fact, I was quite amused to see him dip into his deep pockets to fish out so little money. I felt sad for him because he was struggling financially in those days.

When I entered my home in Balavana as a new bride, it was full of children I had to care for. Karanth was already running a residential school for orphaned children. The responsibility of managing Balavana and taking care of those orphan children were squarely on my shoulders. Therefore, I experienced motherhood well before having my own children.

Karanth had to travel to Mangalore to supervise the printing of the volumes of his encyclopaedia for children, *Bala Prapancha*.[32]

---

32   See B-27 in Annotated Bibliography for more details

He came home only on weekends. Therefore, right from the beginning, I got used to staying alone in Balavana. When Karanth was in Puttur, we often visited his mentor Molahalli Shiva Rao's place. This was the only real outing I had after I came to Balavana.

Money was always a problem. But Karanth had the immense zeal to work and even to earn some money. That zeal was enough for me. He did not have material wealth, but that was okay by me. However, he did have substantial wealth in the form of his good friends. When I thought of our friends, I felt proud of our riches. The responsibility to protect these treasured friendships turned out to be not always easy.

Amma in Balavana after her marriage to Tata

Amma was a great source of support to Tata in those early days when he had not yet gained fame and stature. He was just this crazy genius, a creative man. Amma was often alone in the six-acre patch of semi-wilderness called Balavana. They had very little money. Amma used to say, 'I was a very good cook, but there was nothing in the kitchen or the storeroom to make something nice.'

Amma sustained Tata through that very difficult phase of his life. In the first edition of his autobiography, there is an acknowledgement from Tata about the difficult life she endured for him.[33] He describes those days:

> My burden of loans from previous ventures was weighing on us and lack of money became a constant worry. Leela had to manage the household including her sisters who had come to live with us after her father's death. Such a young girl, who should have been enjoying a carefree life, had to sacrifice many comforts, and stifle her aspirations because she got entangled with me. My insensitive mind may not even have noticed all this. I am a short-tempered, coarse man, always lost in my own thoughts. It may have been hard for her to live with me. But she had never expressed it. Perhaps because she was so young and resilient, she developed her own talents and needs to adapt to the hardships of a life with me.

### *Amma in Balavana: the early years*

The three musketeers in Puttur: Sunanda Baliga,
Amma and Molahalli Sharada Bai

---

33   See B-1 in Annotated Bibliography for more details

Sunanda Baliga, close to Amma in age, became her close friend. Sunanda was from a sophisticated, wealthy Gouda Saraswat family. Her husband Narayana Baliga was a young upcoming lawyer in Puttur. She was genuinely interested in social work even in those days before such an activity turned into a full-time profession for many.

Sunanda Baliga recalled her memories of Amma in Puttur, during the difficult years when the tumultuous events of the Second World War impacted the globe, touching everyone's life:[34]

As a newly married bride, I first came to Puttur on 26 April 1939. Then it became my hometown. After some days, my husband and I visited the Birumale Gudde hill, which is a favoured picnic spot in Puttur. We also ended up visiting Balavana nearby, the place where the well-known writer Shivarama Karanth lived, and kept a menagerie of wild animals. That was our first meeting with Shivarama Karanth and his wife Leela. After that, whenever Leela and I used to meet, we conversed a lot. Our acquaintance turned into a deep friendship during the years that followed. Karanth used to come to Puttur town every day. Sometimes Leela also came with him and visited me.

Leela's generosity and good nature attracted all of us to her. She pitied the needy and would donate money to them, but secretly. She never wanted her charity to be publicised to gain popularity. She was never interested in publicity. She took good care of her household, as Karanth's wife and the mother of their children. To me, Leela was like an elder sister—a true friend, philosopher and guide.

Molahalli Shiva Rao was a leading lawyer and a well-known public figure in Puttur. He once called Leela and me and requested us to raise some funds to renovate the building of the Girls' Primary School, which was in a very dilapidated state. Because of the

---

34   See B-24 in Annotated Bibliography for more details

ongoing Second World War, Sharada Bai, Shiva Rao's married daughter, had also come down from Rangoon, to stay with her parents. The three of us moved around town together. People called us 'the three musketeers'. We formed a committee to support the school. Under the leadership of Leela, we raised quite a bit of money for the school from the tickets we sold of the three plays of Karanth that we staged: *Kisagothami*, *Buddhodaya* and *Nadumaneyalli*. Leela acted in all of them.

Sunanda Baliga continued with her passion for social work, being involved in running an orphanage in Malleshwaram, Bangalore well into her eighties.

From those early days in Puttur, Amma found another lifelong friend and sage counsellor. She was a widowed Gouda Sarawat lady, whom everyone knew only as 'Jeni Amma'. Her two daughters, Shankari Bhat, who was Amma's age, and Leela Bhat, a few years younger, also became her close friends. Leela Bhat, a professor of Kannada, later edited a commemorative book on Amma.[35]

## 'Balonthamma': the Amma of Balavana

Amma, whose compassion for everyone permeated Balavana

---

35   See B-24 in Annotated Bibliography for more details

Amma spent the most important years of her life in Balavana. Whoever came to Balavana never returned empty-handed. Those who came there hungry never returned on an empty stomach. The doors of our house were always open. Amma's life was an open book. She was a free soul. She had no fears and nothing to hide. She was not afraid of anybody or even society. At the same time, she never hurt anyone. She was never jealous. There were many visitors to Balavana, rich and famous, writers and artists—as well as the so-called 'les misérables' of the society. They were all treated and fed in the same way.

Amma's friendly nature transcended all barriers of caste, creed and status. Among her closest friends was a poor Muslim lady who suffered a great deal taking care of her schizophrenic son who had to be kept chained because he occasionally turned violent. We had nicknamed her 'Mailu Kallu Byarthi' (Milestone Byari lady: Byari being the name of a Kanara Muslim community) because her house was next to a milestone. Another similar friend was a Roman Catholic lady with half a dozen children who we named 'Golikatte Bayamma' (Catholic lady of the banyan tree). Right next to her home was a giant banyan tree.

When Amma came to Balavana, Carmina Martis—known as Carimin Bai—had joined us as a domestic help. She worked for several years with our family. In our home, far removed from any neighbours, her six children were playmates to all three of us before we joined high school. Her second daughter, Cecilia, a couple of years younger than Malavika, came to Balavana to help Amma raise Ullas and Kshama, and later, to care for Amma during her ill health, with great devotion. When Malavika raised Svapna and Sharad much later, Cecilia was there for her.

Amma was a truly compassionate humanist. Many poor people would come to Balavana in the evenings while she would be sitting on the 'jagali' (veranda). They would talk to her about all their problems and struggles of existence. When Kshama was young, she did not understand all this and kept getting irritated with this endless stream of people coming to Balavana and crying out for help. But Amma had immense patience. One such friend was Akku, a poor widowed woman who supported her sick parents while working as a daily wage labourer. Malavika nicknamed Akku 'the pathetic friend' because of her endless stories of misery.

Amma once took Kshama along with her on such a mission of mercy. The little girl could not be left alone in Balavana. Kshama remembers it vividly:

> Akku's father had died. Amma had rushed to help her arrange his cremation. Akku had no money. There lay Akku's ripe old father, almost like a bundle of flesh with festering wounds all over him. Amma went around and organised his cremation. Kshama just sat there, stunned. She did not understand why Amma was doing all this. As Kshama's heart and mind matured, she started understanding her mother better. Amma was so deeply compassionate. That is what gave her the strength necessary to face her own challenges.

Narayana Manjeshwara (also see chapter 5) recalls his very first encounter with Amma, years before he joined Tata's service:

> When I was a little boy, I was once walking back home past the Kallimaru Bridge. It was getting dark, and the rain started pouring, totally drenching me. I was carrying home some smelly fish hanging on a string in my hand. A kind-looking lady was walking down the road with an open umbrella. She suddenly asked me, a perfect stranger, to come under her open umbrella. I told her I was carrying these rather smelly fish, and, so could not share her umbrella. But she insisted and took me under her umbrella. She walked with me to my home in that pouring rain and then left. I realised only years later that the kind lady who took me home was the 'Amma of Balavana' whom people spoke about.

Another event witnessed by Kshama and Ullas:

> 'Mad Akku' was a mentally ill woman who used to drop by occasionally at Balavana to beg for some money or food. Without

having had a bath for months, she was stinking to the high heavens. Her long hair had matted and turned brown, caked with dirt. Amma had asked, 'Akku don't you ever have a bath?' Akku had rudely responded, 'Who will give me a bath, will you?' Amma said 'yes' without a moment's hesitation. She took Akku to the bathroom, washed her hair and gave her a thorough bath. She then draped Akku in a fresh clean saree and fed her a hot meal. All of us watching were stunned by her actions. Akku started weeping. She said, '*Amma eer deveru, eer naramani atthu,*' in Tulu. (Amma, you are God. You are not a human being.) Akku fell at Amma's feet and continued weeping.

## *Conversations with Amma: Girija Kulal*

Girija Kulal (1935-2015) was a newly trained teacher in her twenties who first came to Balavana to work as a scribe for Tata. She remained a lifelong loyal friend of our family. She taught basic mathematics to Ullas and Kshama during their homeschooling phase. Years later, when Amma went through her bouts of depression, Girija would come and stay in Balavana as her companion. Girija gradually became part of our family and had many intimate and intense conversations with Amma.

Girija Kulal: 'The teacher' with Ullas, Kshama and
Malavika in the late 1950s

Girija later wrote a brilliant article in Kannada in which she cites some very illuminating conversations she had with Amma, which focused on her life and relationship with Tata.[36] We have translated some excerpts from these conversations here.

Girija Kulal opens with an introduction:

During our conversations, Leelamma narrated many remarkable incidents in her life. She was a great storyteller. She would employ the right facial expressions, body movements and voice modulation to make her narrative come alive with much humour. When she was in full flow, time just flew, and I just listened.

Leelamma was an unforgettable personality. Her mind was pure, simple and almost childlike. I was amazed at how she had decided to marry a man like Karanth with such a lack of concern for her own future. At that time Karanth had no regular income and he was not yet a successful writer. Her marriage to him was not a carefully thought through event: it showed her deep love for him as well as for his artistic genius. By marrying him, Leelamma infused much beauty and happiness into Karanth's solitary life of a wanderer.

Standing beside Karanth, Leelamma gave him the strength he needed to face his battles. Her sacrifices provided the backdrop to his subsequent rise to fame. She struggled to support his most daring ventures, often suppressing her own remarkable talents. Leelamma was substantially responsible for the fame that Karanth attained later. She had to ignore her interests after she married him. However, she has never once claimed to be the architect of his achievements.

In this context, Girija cites Amma's self-effacing words:

I am just an ordinary woman. Like any other woman, I have provided friendship, collaboration and happiness to my husband.

---

36    See B-24 in Annotated Bibliography for more details

His talents are his own, bestowed by God. A crow will always be a crow and cannot be compared to a peacock.

Girija continues:

In his later years Shivarama Karanth was often publicly felicitated by his fans in great style. Although Leelamma attended these events when her fragile health permitted, she usually sat in the audience. She never tried to share the spotlight on stage with her illustrious husband.

Early in his career, however, when Karanth took up new projects, recklessly ignoring the financial risks involved, Leelamma was often worried and anxious. When Karanth worked on his monumental work, the popular science encyclopaedia, *Vijnana Prapancha* he had borrowed thousands of rupees to cover the publication costs.[37]

Karanth always used to share his plans and actions in detail with Leelamma. That was their routine at the end of every day. Although she too was excited by this new project, the fear of sinking ever deeper into debt began bothering her enormously.

Girija describes one such incident narrated by Amma:

One day, when we were chatting on our verandah in Balavana, a lorry fully laden with rolls of printing paper arrived. At the sight of that lorry, I had told Karanth that it scares me witless. An ordinary lorry scared me to death! As Karanth took on bigger and bigger projects, taking huge loans, I got more and more scared. I was worried about the future of our children.

At bedtime, for an hour or so, Karanth confides to me about his financial woes and other difficulties. I listen to him in a daze. Yet I cannot compel myself to tell him to desist from such risky

---

37  See B-28 in Annotated Bibliography for more details

adventures. After unburdening himself, within five minutes, Karanth is in deep slumber and snoring. However, his words of anxiety start echoing inside me. I spend the entire night with my eyes wide open, haunted by his worries.

Girija says, 'At that time they had faced the greatest financial risks of their life. However, they did finally overcome these challenges.'

Girija characterises Amma: 'Leelamma was absolutely fearless. There were many days and nights when Karanth was away travelling, and she had to be alone in Balavana, surrounded by hills and forests, but no neighbours next door.'

As Amma had explained to Girija: 'The books and magazines were my only companions after the experimental school at Balavana was closed down a few months after my arrival. I was quite happy to observe the wild plants and birds around me and to read books quietly. I felt neither fear nor boredom. After my son Harsha was born, time passed even more easily.'

Girija recalls: 'In their home, the doors were never bolted shut, even when Karanth was away travelling. Initially, I was unable to fall asleep, with all those unlocked doors. I once requested Leelamma to keep the doors latched for our own safety. She had replied, "What are you afraid of, Girija? Afraid of thieves? No thieves will come here. They all know there is nothing valuable to steal in Karanth's home. Any thief who comes here will go back miserably disappointed! You can go to sleep peacefully."'

Amma had then laughed, pointing at her son's drawings of tigers: 'These tigers drawn by Ullas will guard us.'

Girija recounts:

The two little children, Ullas and Kshama, sleeping next to us, had also joined her in teasing me about my fears. My fears eventually subsided.

Such lightheartedness was Leelamma's natural trait. Not just of hers, but that of the entire Karanth family. Yes, she was right! There were Ullas' tigers and were only on paper. Even as a little boy, Ullas drew beautiful pictures of tigers in different postures—hunting, jumping and eating other animals. He would leave these drawings all over the place. It is such a pleasure for me to see that little Ullas now being engaged in the big task of saving real tigers.

My connection with the Karanth family has endured for over forty years. The first fifteen years of my professional life were spent at Balavana. I have witnessed and experienced happiness as well as the sorrow of the Karanth family from close quarters. I was also fortunate to enjoy their unique affection. If they all sat together to talk, I too joined in the mirth, so much that we often got exhausted by all that laughing.

When Shivarama Karanth was among children, he too became a child. He was like a wiser older friend to any child he met. Most of the times, Karanth used to address his own children using funny nicknames that he affectionately coined for them.

After Karanth finished his work for the day, as he came down the stairs from his study, he used to affectionately call out to Leelamma, addressing her as 'O La'. He would ask her for a glass of water and drink it up before going on his routine evening walk to the town. When Karanth bantered with his children about their mother, he jokingly referred to her 'Ammade', which is how the name 'Ahmed' plays out on Tulu tongues. Leelamma also used to banter with Karanth. Instead of going up the stairs to his office, she would mischievously call out to him from below, addressing him as 'Hoy Karanthare'.

When their little children, Ullas and Kshama, quarrelled and called out to him to resolve some silly dispute of theirs, Karanth used to take a break from his work, and come downstairs. He rarely got angry with his children, even when they disturbed him at work.

Leelamma soon faced an additional worry. She had to take care of her aged grandmother Mallappe who had moved to Balavana in 1958 (from her son Gopala Alva's home in Puttur). She needed to be physically cared for like an infant because of her frail health and advanced senility. Leelamma stood guard over her all night long, losing much sleep. She had great affection for her grandmother, who had taken such tender care of her, and her sisters, after they had lost their mother.

Leelamma's mental health became precarious between 1959-60, after bearing the strain of caring for Mallappe. It deteriorated further, with the death of her favourite son Harsha in 1961.

Leelamma did not weep publicly before the people who came to console her after she lost Harsha. She would calmly describe the suffering Harsha had endured in his last days, and then went on to say, 'There are many other mothers in this world who also have lost their sons. Now it is my turn. These are our "prarabdha karmas" (the consequences of our wrongdoings in our previous births).' The visitors wondered at her emotional strength. Some even shed tears when she calmly continued, 'Many young men visit Balavana even now. I see the image of my Harsha in all of them. As far as I am concerned, they are all my Harsha.'

Although she put on a brave front, Harsha's death had deeply wounded her. Years after Amma's death, among her papers, Malavika found a handwritten poem addressed to Harsha.[38]

Going well beyond her family, Leelamma had woven bonds of human love around Balavana. It encompassed everyone around her: the family, domestic help, the driver, the workers in the press were all her people. When they were happy, she too was. To Tuluva villagers in the neighbourhood, Leela Karanth became 'Balonthamma'.

---

38   See Appendix-2 for the English translation of the poem

Normally Leelamma conversed with the locals in Tulu, employing pithy embellishments in the form of jokes, aphorisms and adages found in abundance in that beautiful language. These villagers came to Leelamma feeling unhappy, spoke their hearts out, got useful guidance and sometimes practical assistance, and then after a meal or snacks, they went back feeling much better.

Poor school students occasionally came to Balavana seeking help or guidance. Too scared to meet Karanth, they first talked to Leelamma. She spoke to them with motherly affection, gave them some food, and then took them upstairs to meet Karanth. If he was not home, she would give them whatever money she had on her. Thereafter, she sent them off to seek additional help from her charitable friends in Puttur. Many such students who she blessed in this manner later returned to Balavana during their holidays, often spending a couple of days with her. Years later even, after they had acquired advanced education, decent jobs, got married, and had children, they would keep coming back to visit Leelamma. All of them seemed to feel they too were her children.

'Leelamma's loving voice, filled with empathy, permeated the entire Karanth home. It still haunts me. I think I will keep hearing that voice forever,' says Girija Kulal at the end of her narrative.

One of the students mentioned in Girija's account above is Ganapathy Joisa, a poor but bright student who went on to study mining engineering at the Banaras Hindu University in the 1950s with Tata's financial support. Ullas and Kshama used to look forward to his annual visits to Balavana. Joisa was a superb storyteller, translating Bram Stoker's *Dracula* into Kannada for them in a hair-raising manner.

## *Tata and Amma: The great journey*

Amma and Tata, performing in a dance-drama

Amma has written about Tata thus:

Karanth is Karnataka's treasure. A great source of wealth. His efforts to attain that status are beyond one's imagination. His writings express his brilliance, his inborn gifts and how he built on these with his hard work. Let that great energy, working with the same focus, even today at his advanced age flourish among our people for a hundred more years. This is possible because of his good health. Though he works like a labourer while at home, he loves travelling also. New places and new people provide him with fresh energy and enthusiasm. At the same time, these travels also provide the rest he needs to recover from the burdens of his hard work. If not for these rest periods and change of scenery, his work would have defeated him. His Karma Yoga which starts in the morning ends only when he goes to bed in the night. He is a real Yogi. He is a superhuman. He has achieved whatever he aimed at with great dedication, undaunted by difficulties he has faced. We are so lucky to have him amongst us.

He is fortunate too. Many people with great intellect are not backed by the lady luck in their lives, and, obstacles have the upper hand. That did not happen with Karanth. He faced difficulties during the first half of his life, whereas in the second half things went quite well for him. It was good that he struggled during the first half. It made him mature fully. At a younger age, he had the ability to absorb the blows life dealt him. Others, who are too weak to withstand such hardships, collapse and get sidelined in life. However, Karanth regenerates new aspirations and sets new goals, even while undergoing disappointments. No difficulty or sorrow shakes him. His basic mantra is his work. Once he delves into his work, there is nothing in his mind. His life revolves around his work.

Karanth is an admirer of all the beauty around him. He is a simple man. Nothing makes him feel arrogant or proud, not even money. What he feels in a particular situation may be different from how any of us would feel. He can experience special, strange emotions. His feeling of sorrow, hardships, difficulty or happiness is far more intense than in others. We can't fathom the depths of that rare mind. Karanth himself is not aware of what an asset his mind is. Only god, the creator, is aware of that. The good wishes of the people, their prayers for Karanth, do bear fruit. We may not find this kind of a person anywhere else in this world. It is our pride that such a person is ours. Although Karanth appears to be like one of us, only Karanth can be Karanth.

Amma and Tata in Balavana; the years of harmony

In her essay, 'Naa Kanda Karantha' (The Karanth I Saw)[39] Amma offers a more nuanced perspective of Tata. Here, inter alia, Amma says, 'This Karanth is not a real person. He is a gifted actor. His entire life is an enactment by that actor. No real individual could have lived this way and accomplished so much in a single lifetime.'

Amma and Tata in Saligrama: while Tata flourishes, Amma declines

---

39   See B-26 in Annotated Bibliography for more details

Kshama vividly recalls visiting Balavana eleven years after Amma's death. She recalls that moment in her own words:

As I sat in the corner of the Verandah, peace descended on me. This is where Amma used to sit. A very compassionate person, her words brought solace to many a suffering soul. She did not discriminate between the poor and the rich. She was a brave lady who stood by my father in his early struggles, made many sacrifices so that he could realise his dreams. His brave companion and wife, she could not share much of the joy of his later successes because by then she had been reduced to a mere shadow of her former self due to afflictions of the body and mind. But Tata had marched ahead, alone, with his indomitable courage.

In all this great migration of human beings across the vast expanse of life, those who are sick, old and weak, will falter and fall, unable to swim across the mighty river. Those who reach the other shore emerge stronger and successful. Tata reached the other shore and achieved spectacular success. Amma failed, but won the hearts of one and all with her great empathy, love, deep spirituality and honesty.

# 3

# A LITTLE GIRL GROWS UP IN BALAVANA

*Malavika Kapur*

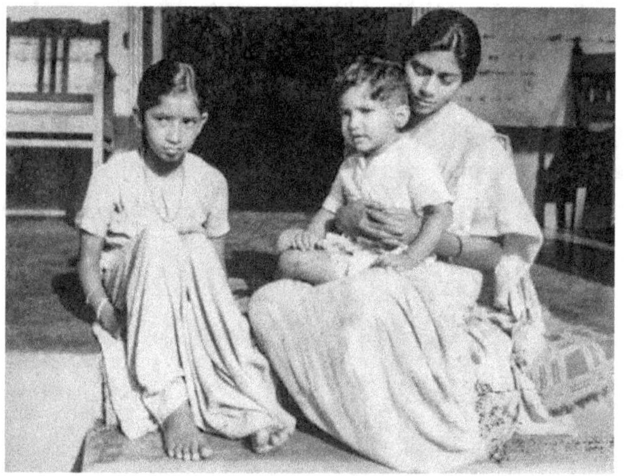

A little girl in Balavna: Malavika, with Varija,
a relative of Amma, holding Ullas

## My childhood

I would like to go back to my memories of Tata in chronological order as they unfolded in my life. There are two clear parts to my life: the first sixteen years that I spent in Balavana as a child and an adolescent. Then the events in my life after I grew up and moved out of Balavana. In these two successive chapters that cover these parts, I will highlight how my experiences have shaped me.

I was always called 'Malu' by my parents. My earliest memory is of Tata carrying me in his arms while on his walks. Tata walked from Balavana to Puttur town twice a day—a total distance of twelve kilometres. The first walk in the morning was to the post office; again at four in the evening Tata would walk to a large shop on the main street owned by his friend Shridhar Bhat. On the evening walk, he carried me to town. Tata and a small group of friends sat there chatting for an hour or so. I would be playing around in the shop, listening to them talk without understanding a word. Tata returned home by 6.30 p.m. I greatly enjoyed those regular outings to the town.

Once, when we were coming back, Tata was feeling feverish. He told me, 'Malu, I can't carry you today because I feel very tired. Instead, can you lead me on the way home today?' Saying that, he extended his little finger to me. I held on to it, and moved ahead of him on the way back home, supremely confident that I was leading him back. From that day onward, I insisted on walking with him, rather than being carried. Those long evening walks, continually chit-chatting with Tata, were one of the nicest things in my life when I was a little girl.

Another incident I recall is of me having high fever, and going without a bath for several days. When I recovered, my hair was all matted up. Amma tried to untangle it with a comb, which was so painful that I started screaming. Tata was busy at work in his upstairs study. But he rushed down, lifted me up and pacified me. With his nimble fingers, he untangled each one of those knots. It took him half an hour, but he did it without hurting me at all. Tata always had great difficulty looking at any human being in pain.

Every afternoon, after a short nap, Tata routinely drank a cup of hot tea. I used to go up to his study, eager for a sip of tea. He would pour a little tea for me, and I was quite happy. One day, for no reason at all, I pestered him for more and more tea! Tata lost his temper and poured the entire cup of tea over my head. I was very humiliated and started to cry. He lifted me and took me to the bathroom and washed and dried my hair. His anger rose fast, but also subsided just as quickly.

The best thing that happened during the day was a ritual we enacted just before bedtime. At about eight in the evening, Tata would tell me a story. That story would go on for about an hour. He would give me a choice on the theme of the day's story. I could, for example, say, 'Today I want a story in which there is *ondu rajakumari, ondu rakshasa, ondu kaadu*' (a princess, an ogre, and a jungle). Tata would then begin to spin the entire tale in the next instant. His creativity and spontaneity were incredible.

Ullas was born eight years after me, and Kshama, after ten. This gave me eight years of complete monopoly over Tata's company. I ordered him to come up with new stories daily and remember smiling in anticipation about the day's story. These are some of my happiest memories of those years.

After a story ended, sometimes Tata would say, 'Who is going to press my feet, which are so sore?' After long hours of dance training, or walking, his feet would indeed be sore. I always jumped at the opportunity to massage his feet and afterwards ask him, 'How was the massage today?' He would smile and say, 'Malu, it felt like a breeze blowing over roses!' I rejoiced, although I did not understand what he meant.

Tata's printing press was called Harsha Printery, named after my elder brother. One day I asked Tata, 'Why is the press named Harsha Printery? Is there nothing named after Malu?' He instantly responded jokingly, saying, 'Harsha Printery, Malu Kurlari' (in Tulu, puffed rice is called 'kurlari'). I was very upset and demanded, '*Naanu yaake kurlari?*' (Why are you calling me merely puffed rice?)

A few days later, when Tata launched a new series of short stories for children, he called the series *Malavika Kathamaale* (Malavika's Garland of Stories). He had made amends for blowing off my concern about the printing press being named after my brother. He would sometimes make a remark lightly, but later think about it and act seriously. Many lovely stories for children were brought out by Tata under this new series named after me. I was fully satisfied!

In fact, this series of stories got me interested in writing fiction.

During the day, when I was alone in Balavana in my younger years, I had no playmates or companions. Sometimes I used to go up to Tata and asked him to make a doll for me. He would get hold of some cardboard, coloured crepe paper, and all sorts of other materials to make that doll for me.

Tata had, in his youth, got himself a crude tattoo on his forearm. It depicted Krishna playing the flute. That tattoo fascinated me.

Sometimes Tata created fully illustrated storybooks for me. They were full of colours and action, but the central theme was always decided by me. I did not have to buy children's comic books, because Tata was creating them at home. Soon, I too was making my own dolls and illustrations. Although I was alone, I did not feel lonely. Balavana was surrounded by woods and I was happy being creative and playing all alone in them.

After I picked up my reading skills, when I was about ten, I had told Tata, 'Now that I can read, you don't have to spin your stories for me every night. You can now start telling your stories to Ullas and Kshama.' I did not feel that my younger siblings competed with me. I was ready to move on in life and do my own thing.

My childhood was a very happy time. Not all adults can say they had the happiest of childhoods. I would consider my childhood as the happiest period in my life.

Amma would teach me some basic skills in math or reading, for a short time each day. Or she would take out an encyclopaedia and show me the pictures in it, explaining in detail what they were. Tata nurtured my creative side, Amma the practical side. She helped me gain useful skills.

Tata was a very significant influence in my life. I can look back and say I was totally pampered by Tata. I was a spoilt brat. If I asked for something, I usually got it. I felt I could twist Tata around my little finger. I continued to be Tata's spoilt, favourite child till I was about ten, when Kshama was born.

As a part of his daily activities, Tata used to dabble a lot with paints and dyes to create makeup, costumes and other props for the plays he staged. Consequently, his fingers were often stained with paint and ink. Therefore, Tata always used a spoon to eat his meals, unlike the rest of our family that ate using fingers.

Tata used to be a heavy smoker those days. He stopped smoking when India's finance minister, Morarji Desai, imposed steep tax hikes on cigarettes in the late Fifties. Tata ate very small meals and loved to drink strong coffee. I believe his small meals, long walks and physical activity contributed to his longevity. But it was his childlike curiosity that made him what he was. His tireless persistence and energy were the source of his creativity.

I remember that once a friend of his, a devout person, offered some 'vibhuti prasada' (sacred ash) to Tata. Preoccupied, Tata mistook the sacred ashes to be snuff. He snorted it all up, much to the chagrin of that god-fearing friend! I had great fun watching such goof-ups when I was with Tata.

Tata loved to use puns a lot when he cracked jokes. I would groan at these dreadful puns. Once my cousin Ramamohan (son of Sridevi Sadashiva Rao, Tata's sister) asked Tata why our home was named Balavana. Employing one of his puns, Tata replied that it was because Tata had a 'bala' (tail in Kannada). Truly believing him, for a while, all my cousins used to call him 'Balada Mava', or the uncle with a tail.

If there were any mischievous boys around, Tata would brand them as 'Hanumantha Raya' (after the god Hanuman in Ramayana, who had allegedly burned down Ravana's capital city, Lanka, by monkeying around with a blazing torch tied to his tail).

Usually whatever I said was accepted by Tata without question. I used to be very talkative, persistent, argumentative and stubborn with him. Exasperated, he would call me 'Be-bi-Be, Bennu Bidada Betala' (the monster that will not get off my back)!

When I was about five years old, Tata asked me, 'Do you want to start learning to read and write now?'

I had replied, 'No, no, no, I want a long holiday. Give me one more year of holiday.' He had agreed without imposing his will on me.

When I started high school, I discovered that I was capable of being independent. I started acting all grown up. Novels and stories became my lifeline. I went on to read a lot in Kannada, and later in English. I recall reading four or five books every week, something I continue to do even now. My eclectic reading habit arose out of stories that I had heard from Tata in my childhood.

No more a little girl: Tata and Malavika at home

Looking back, growing up as a little girl in Balavana was a fascinating experience. Many people from varied professions visited Tata for different purposes. There were so many visitors that local people compared our home to a 'chathra' (a choultry that provided free lodging and board). Occasionally, a drama or dance troupe would arrive in Balavana without any notice to Amma. She then had to cook food for twenty or more people. Tata offered them hospitality, without much thought about how difficult it would be for Amma to manage things at such short notice.

## *Tata's friends, the literary giants*

Of course, there were also many distinguished invited guests, including the literary giants of Kannada like Da. Ra. Bendre, Masti Venkatesha Iyengar, V. Seetharamaiah ('Vee. See.'), and such others. There used to be a star-shaped lily pond in the centre of our front yard. Because of water scarcity Tata had got the pond filled up to create a platform. Tata and his distinguished visitors would sit on that star-shaped platform and discuss literature, fine arts and whatever else that interested them. Those literary giants were more like companions than the present set who are more like competitors. They were all good friends of Tata—Vee. See., Masti and Sriranga (R.V. Jahagirdar). They were all like my uncles. I remember sitting behind Tata and trying to braid his longish hair while he was in deep discussions with them. I was having my own fun. The literary discussions underway were beyond my comprehension. (Years later, Sriranga's daughter, the noted writer Shashi Deshpande, and I became very good friends.)

Tata would continue with his daily routine of writing, even when we had such guests. He would come down to join them for meals and go back upstairs to work. It was Amma who kept them engaged. She was quite an intellectual companion to some of these literary figures. She was also the perfect hostess.

I remember Amma discussing serious literary and philosophical issues with some of these guests. What I remember most vividly was a huge pile of correspondence dating back to before the 1940s, between Amma and the eminent writer and philosopher D.V. Gundappa (DVG). These exchanges were conducted when DVG was writing his magnum opus, *Manku Thimmana Kagga*.

These literary figures came to Balavana to visit Tata but they bonded with our whole family. They stayed on because of Amma. She was the magnet that drew everybody to Balavana.

Two other good friends of Tata in Bangalore, who I knew as a girl of eight, were M. Shivaram (Raa. Shi.), a reputed physician in Malleshwaram, and K.V. Iyer, a famed bodybuilder who had established the gymnasium called Vyayama Shala on J.C. Road.

I remember acting in a production of Tata's dance-drama, *Lava–Kusha*, with many other children participating. I played the role of Lava. It was staged in the main hall of Vyayama Shala, while being surrounded by weightlifting equipment and life-sized photographs of K.V. Iyer displaying his splendid physique staring down at us from the walls. The great bodybuilder was very fond of me. Because I was a skinny little girl, he used to lift me and exclaim, '*Yelu mallige tookada nanna rajakumari!*' (My princess who is as light as seven jasmine flowers.) I was very pleased with all this flattery.

When Amma suffered some affliction of the liver she was brought to Bangalore for treatment. We stayed in one of the guest rooms at Vyayama Shala. Shivaram was the doctor who took care of Amma for a month or so.

Tata, the doctor and the bodybuilder bonded over Kannada literature. K.V. Iyer was a fine novelist too, with *Shanthala* being a classic for which he is remembered even today. His other novel is *Roopadarshi*, on a theme of Michelangelo creating his famous sculpture of David. I consider it one of the best books I have read in Kannada. What I also vividly recall is being spooked by K.V. Iyer reading out ghost stories to me at bedtime.

Apart from his medical practice, Shivaram had established a superb humour magazine in Kannada, called *Koravanji*. It was modelled after the British humour magazine, *Punch*. The only thing it lacked in comparison was its glossy production. *Koravanji* proved to be the fertile field from which many eminent Kannada humourists sprouted, including the legendary cartoonist R.K. Laxman who began his career at that magazine. When I was growing up, *Koravanji* was one of my favourite magazines.

Shivaram also wrote a series of books on medical practices and therapy. He holistically treated his patients with much empathy, addressing their physical ailments as well as mental health. He wrote three fascinating books, *Manonandana*, *Manamanthana* and

*Ananda.* As a clinical psychologist, I now perceive that Shivaram addressed problems of 'health psychology' and 'lifestyle disorders' that we now recognise. My relationship with Shivaram's family continues even today.

## Experiences with Amma and Tata

Amma's mental illness began when I was only five, when she had her first clear depressive episode. Scarily, she had taken me to the edge of the open well in Balavana and said, 'Malu, we both are going to jump into this well.' Apparently, I had told her, '*Bedaamma, nanage jeevanta irabeku. Nanage saaylikke ishhta illa.*' (No, Amma, I want to live. I don't want to die.) She told me later that I had saved her life. After that strange episode, she was her usual extroverted self for several years.

Amma was affectionate and sociable to a fault. So much so that I used to get embarrassed by her sociability. In a small town like Puttur, she would stop and talk to everyone we met while walking down the main street.

When I was about thirteen, Tata went on his eight-week trip to Europe by steamship. One night, when Tata was away, Amma woke me up suddenly in the middle of the night and said, 'I am being possessed by a Devi (goddess) and you should touch my feet!' This was her second episode of that manic mood I witnessed. I was very afraid again.

When I was around seven years old, one of our domestic helps wanted to leave early because she wanted to buy some magic potion from a wandering 'mantrawadi' vendor. I caustically made fun of her, laughing at her belief in mantras and potions. She was very hurt and started to cry. Amma was very upset with me when she saw the maid crying. She slapped me hard and said, 'This should put an end to your being rude to poor, helpless people who work for us.' That was the only time she ever beat me and the lesson has stayed with me: kindness to the helpless should be our prime concern.

At age ten, I decided to join high school. Tata agreed. However, he did not want me to attend the convent school run by Roman Catholic nuns. Although many middle-class parents opted for it, believing it provided better education in the English medium, Tata had the reservation that these schools tried to covertly preach Christianity. Even in his novel *Chomana Dudi*, Tata is critical of religious conversion of people in depressed Hindu social classes under the inducement of money. However, he was an atheist and the practice of any religion did not matter much to him.

Tata sent me and my siblings to the Kannada medium government school, the Board High School in Puttur. Luckily for me, our school had an enormous library with a large collection of excellent books in both Kannada and English. We had several dedicated teachers and the school had extensive playgrounds and sports facilities. It was a great school, and I did not regret the 'no convent school' decision made by Tata.

I vividly remember the night Kshama was born in 1950. Tata was preparing to leave town the next day, taking his dance-drama troupe on a trip. His team was busy packing up the props and equipment. Suddenly, Amma started having labour pains. Immediately they cleared the room of all materials. They were all packed away quickly. Tata meanwhile got a midwife to come to Balavana to assist in the delivery of the baby. Amma gave birth comfortably.

Early next morning Tata packed his bags and went off with his troupe. At that time this did not seem like odd behaviour to me. The baby was born at night and everybody was up and about, busy taking care of Amma. Amma had never insisted, 'You cannot do this. I need you.' I consider her a wife who gave complete freedom to her husband. I don't think many women can do that. Next morning, I too went off to school happily. I said to myself, if Tata can go on his trip as planned, I too can go to school. The show must go on was the guiding principle of our lives. No matter what happened, you continue doing whatever you had to do.

I think Amma held our family and home together so that Tata was free to do what he wanted. There was much work involved in running the printing press. When Tata took off on his trips, it was Amma who managed the press in addition to running the household.

We were not wealthy, but we lived very comfortably. At no time did I have a feeling that we were deprived in any way. There was always something available to meet basic needs. Amma was able to run the household efficiently and was a gracious hostess with whatever she possessed. We had a constant stream of guests, some invited, some who just dropped in and many others who stayed for days or even weeks.

Amma used to joke with me that I turned out to be a psychologist because she had read Sigmund Freud's work when she was pregnant with me. It was amazing that a nineteen-year-old young woman like her, who was just a matriculate, was not only reading Freud, but fully comprehending him. Amma was a voracious reader with a strong need to seek knowledge.

When I was growing up, the theatre was a very important part of our lives. Amma was a very good actress, dancer and singer. In all of Tata's 'geetha natakas' (dance-dramas), Amma used to play the lead role. I also participated in quite a few of these dance-dramas and operas. We were all part of Tata's experiments.

I remember how Tata created his stage props and trained me in singing and dancing. I also remember how we performed for our school annual day and other functions. Long before the day arrived, we gathered regularly and rehearsed. I would be doing my role and suddenly Tata would get very angry at some mistake. He never struck me, because I was frozen with fear. But it was a rewarding experience to be trained by him in dance, music and drama. Theatre was very important both to me and to Kshama.

When I was in high school, we were performing the geetha nataka, the opera *Lava–Kusha*. I was playing the role of Sita. Suddenly, I was afflicted with laryngitis and entirely lost my voice on the day of the show. Amma said, 'Malu, do not worry. Just lip sync to the lyrics, I will be your playback singer.' That day, Amma gave me her voice so well that everyone thought I was singing. Amma would come up with solutions to problems with such spontaneity. Anyone else would have cancelled the play when the lead character lost her voice, but not my Amma. I even managed to bag the first prize for my role as Sita. Similarly, on another occasion, I came down with measles just before my school exams, and was unable to read because my eyes were burning. Amma read out my textbooks to me so that I could pass the exams. She was so dependable.

I was a very sober girl from a very young age. Amma used to poke fun at me, saying, 'Malu, you are my mother-in-law, not my daughter.' Although I found her cheery exuberance excessive at times, we had a very close relationship.

As far as his work was concerned, Tata was a speed fiend. He wrote most of his novels within a week or two. All his book projects were completed within the deadlines he had set for himself. Procrastination was unknown to him, and he never complained about any 'writer's block'.

Some criticised Tata's attempts to dabble in multiple domains—literature, arts and popular science. The specialists in each field found some flaw or the other. On the other hand, for me, this was an appealing quality in Tata, because he wanted to do so many different things. Each one of those things was as important as the other. As far as I am concerned, whatever one decides to do is important as long as one enjoys it. That's what I have learnt from Tata.

I now go trekking in the Himalayas, I do ceramics, I like to attend theatre, I learn classical music and I write on different genres—fiction and non-fiction, with psychology being my deep passion. I find doing each of these activities more enjoyable than sticking to just a single one. Because that is how Tata also viewed life; he did not pay much attention to his critics. He realised that if he focused on just one thing, he could be perfect in that domain. If he did a hundred different things, he knew he could not be perfect in each one. What I absorbed from him was, 'Do what you enjoy the most. It does not matter if it is not perfect, as long as you enjoy it.'

Tata used to take me along on his travels. These were exciting trips but at times embarrassing too. In one of the mofussil towns, we were watching a locally sponsored cultural event. An adolescent girl came on stage dancing as a 'koravanji' (soothsayer). She wore a very seductive attire and moved around sensuously like an adult. As the girl was dancing, Tata stood up and shouted at the organisers, 'Stop this nonsense! This dance looks so obscene when performed by such a young girl.' There was stunned silence all around. The dance was immediately stopped. I found his public expression of anger very embarrassing at that time.

Tata had always believed that any performing art meant for children had to suit the age of the child. I wonder how offended Tata would be now by the present-day television 'reality shows' performed by children.

Sometimes, listening to his lectures or seeing him teach dance, I found fault with things, which he would acknowledge later. Once when Tata was playing the role of Shoorpanakha in a Ramayana play, displaying all her seductive mannerisms, I was watching from the wings. As he came closer, I saw that the sticking plaster that held down his moustache under the heavy make-up was about to peel off. I loudly whispered to him to come to the wings. He came into the wings, and I quickly fixed his moustache. A seductive Shoorpanakha sporting a bristling moustache would not have worked! We both laughed about this later for days on end.

Amma and I both participated in Tata's theatre experiments. We also used to travel with his dance-drama troupes. As I grew older, when both travelled, I took on more responsibilities in the house and even at the printing press because Amma loved to travel with him if she could.

Amma was a good writer in Kannada. Her name has been listed in a volume on early women writers of South Kanara edited by short story writer Manorama Bhat.[40] The volume contains a fine profile

---

40   See B-23 in Annotated Bibliography for more details

of Amma written by Rekha Bannadi, which cites examples of her literary talents. If she had a greater opportunity to nurture her own talents, undoubtedly, Amma too would have been a reputed writer in her own right.

Amma was fluent in Marathi because she grew up in Bombay. She also used to read Marathi magazines, from which she translated stories for me into Kannada. She had translated Harinarayan Apte's Marathi classic *Pun Lakshat Kon Gheto?* (But Who Cares?) into Kannada with some editorial help from Tata. The Kannada version, *Yaaru Lakshisavaru?*, had both their names on its cover as translators.[41]

When Tata worked on a book, be it fiction or non-fiction, each day he would discuss the progress with all of us after dinner. Once he was laying out the overall theme of his latest novel before us. He said, 'I have given it the title, *Thiddidavaru, Telidavaru*, which roughly means "those who improved others, and the rest who escaped".' I had laughed out loud and teasingly said, 'Why not add *Yemme Karu Kattidavaru* (those who tended the water buffalo calves) to the title to make it sound even more ridiculous?' This led to tremendous mirth, with Amma, Ullas and Kshama too joining me in teasing Tata. Next morning, he had changed the title of that novel to *Sameekshe* (The Overview).[42]

Tata was a doting father to Ullas and Kshama when they were young. Amma told me that he had a more difficult time with my elder brother Harsha. Even as a baby, Harshanna had problems sleeping and was cranky through the night. Tata had to put him on his shoulder and pace up and down for hours just so that Amma could catch some sleep. The problems he had with Harshanna escalated as the years went by (refer to chapter 5).

Until I matriculated from high school, I lived at home. When I was thirteen, girls in my class decided to wear sarees, transitioning from

---

41    See B-29 in Annotated Bibliography for more details
42    See B-30 in Annotated Bibliography for more details

the stage of long skirts and blouses. Tata bought me just four cotton sarees. During the heavy monsoon rains that lash South Kanara, I would walk between home and high school, three kilometres each way. Within three months, all my four sarees were in shreds, because I did not know how to wear them to minimise wear and tear. I went to Tata asking for more sarees. He said, 'I can't afford to buy you four sarees every three months.' I apologised and promised to be more careful. He did buy me new sarees, but this lesson on the virtue of parsimony has stayed with me.

When I visited Mangalore with Tata, at age sixteen, I saw for the first time girls my own age wearing nail polish. When I asked Tata to buy me nail polish, he retorted, 'All that fancy stuff is not for simple people like us, my child.' I remember being very upset. That was the first time I felt constrained by him, but obeyed him unwillingly.

By the time I was in my teens I wanted a puppy as a pet and asked Amma to get me one. She flatly refused, saying, 'Puppies foul up the house quite a lot. I will not get you one.' I still went ahead and wrote to Tata, who happened to be in Bangalore, asking him to bring me a pup. He brought a chocolate brown Spaniel-Dachshund hybrid pup, which I named Jim. Amma was very angry, saying, 'Every bit of the mess this puppy makes, you will have to clean it, Malu. Nobody else will help you because you got it from your Tata, without my consent.' Thereafter, Jim became my sole responsibility. Jim lived in Balavana for the next thirteen years. He slept all day long at Tata's feet when he worked at his desk. Amma as well as Ullas and Kshama came to love Jim.

The lesson I learned was: everything comes to you as both a right and a responsibility.

Finally, having completed my high school education, the day arrived when I had to leave Balavana for college and be on my own. Whatever values my parents had inculcated in me had to be put to the test. I felt I was ready.

# 4

# LIFE AWAY FROM BALAVANA

*Malavika Kapur*

Malavika during her college days

## *My college education: Finding a passion for psychology*

Since I wanted to pursue college education and there were no colleges in Puttur, Tata chose to send me to Mahatma Gandhi Memorial (MGM) College in Udupi. It was a very good college, where Tata's friend K.S. Haridas Bhat was my professor. The teachers at MGM College were all excellent, and the college had a great library. But there was no residential hostel for girls.

I finally ended up renting a room for myself in the home of a Bunt family. I had not yet learned to cook. I had a very hard time adjusting to that environment because the family was rather dysfunctional. Although I was writing to Tata and Amma every week about the good things I was doing at college, I did not dare to share my domestic difficulties. Even during the vacations that I spent in Balavana, I maintained my silence, worried that they would discontinue my college education.

After I completed a year of pre-university education in Udupi, I shared my difficulties with my parents and requested them to get me admission to the undergraduate programme in the Government Arts and Science College in Mangalore. Because of our old family connections to Besant High School, I hoped I could stay in the hostel of that school. Fortunately, this plan worked out and rebuilt my self-confidence.

In the first year of my BA, I chose the then radically new subject of psychology. Gowrishankar Prabhu, a brilliant teacher, had sparked my interest in psychology. Years later, we became colleagues in Bangalore. But after I had completed my first year, Prabhu left Mangalore. If I had continued my education in Mangalore, I could not have continued my studies in psychology. The only option to pursue my passion was in the faraway city of Mysore. However, I told myself, 'If you know what you want to do in life, you must try hard to get it. You can't expect others to solve your problems, even if they are your parents.'

The other good thing going my way was, unlike most girls my age, I was not being pressured to get married by my parents. Amma would occasionally suggest that I should think about getting married to 'a nice young man, whoever he is'. She would even try to point out 'suitable boys'. I brushed her aside, saying, 'Why this preoccupation with my marriage? I don't want to get married. I want to be independent.'

A year later, I boldly set forth to join the Maharani's College in Mysore to continue my undergraduate studies in psychology. Each month Tata would send me a small stipend of 40 rupees—36 rupees for my hostel expenses and only four rupees for any personal expenses. I became very frugal. Tata liked the fact that I was studious, frugal and decidedly conventional.

Although Tata was a very liberal father in some ways, he could also be stubbornly conservative. These attitudes were obvious when I was in Mysore. I wanted to join the extracurricular student paramilitary organisation, the National Cadet Corps (NCC), which had just been introduced. All my college friends had volunteered to participate. However, Tata flatly refused me permission with the diktat: 'No! I don't like the idea of girls wearing pants.' I was very envious of my friends wearing pants in the NCC.

After completing my bachelor's degree in psychology, Tata encouraged me to pursue my passion by enrolling in the master's degree programme at the Manasa Gangothri campus of the University of Mysore. We were only two girls among eight students in that class. The famous Professor Kuppuswamy was my teacher. We had to conduct practical experiments on human subjects, forming smaller groups. Because we were only two girls, these groups were necessarily mixed.

A couple of months later, a professor of philosophy who was a friend of my uncle, K.R. Karanth, wrote to Tata that I was overly friendly with the boys in my class. Tata, with his usual penchant for sending cryptic telegrams, sent one that just said, 'Come home immediately.' I took the overnight bus from Mysore and reached Balavana in the morning. Tata confronted me with the offending letter, saying, 'A professor has complained that you are talking to the boys in your class!'

I was furious. I retorted, saying, 'We are two girls. We must conduct experiments in teams that include boys. I can't participate in experiments without talking to the boys. Either you let me go back and study or stop my education. You cannot tell me that I can go back and study psychology without talking to boys in my class.' My strong ultimatum made him realise how foolish he had been. He sheepishly said, 'Go back, go back. Do whatever you want to do.'

There was a very strong, caring, trusting relationship between us. I had fought back with facts, and Tata respected that. He never brought up the subject of boys again.

In contrast, Amma had total faith in me. I could not do anything wrong. 'Let Malu do what she wants,' was her clear opinion. Tata's judgement of people was much poorer than Amma's. Even if a stranger wrote something nonsensical to him, he had this tendency to believe the worst first and ask questions later.

## Harshanna's death

Harshanna: formal portrait of a troubled youth

When I was studying in Mysore, Harshanna tragically died at the age of twenty-three. It was a major crisis in our family, especially for Amma.

Harshanna's last days in Bombay are best recounted by Tata's good friend, Ganesh Bhat, a professor of chemistry in IIT Bombay.

Tata teasingly called him 'mooka sakshi' (the mute witness). He was one of Tata's close friends. Although Bhat greatly admired Tata, he could also be critical of some of Tata's flaws. (After Bhat retired, he returned home to Malpe village near Udupi and stayed in touch with Tata and me.)

Bhat recalls Tata's visits to Bombay. 'Now, instead of Karanth's usual visits on work, he had come to deal with his son's illness. Unfortunately, Harsha had developed a malignant lymphatic sarcoma. Karanth knew it was a serious condition. Harsha was getting breathless and bloated. This cancer required urgent surgical removal.'

Tata wrote a letter to me dated 23 January 1961 while staying in Ganesh Bhat's room in Sharada Bhavan Hotel in Bombay. The letter was in Kannada and I have translated it below:

To Malu,

… your brother's illness is very serious. After the x-rays, the decision to surgically intervene has become essential. Since the last 15 days, he (Harsha) is suffering a great deal. Doctors Baliga and Shah will operate on him in another couple of days. What lies ahead is in the hands of chance. I am writing this so that you know why we all need to be prepared to face very difficult situations, death and pain in all our lives. Whenever these come into our lives we must experience and suffer our share of it.

Yesterday, I saw your brother in the hospital and came back to my room. He is astonishingly brave about it. I hope it stays this way tomorrow as well.

*Your mother is staying with her friend Molahalli Sharada Bai. I don't know what pain is in store for her. If something untoward happens here, I will send you a telegram. Please go home straightaway and be with the children. I feel sad when I think of just two of them there (Ullas and Kshama in Puttur).*

*Here I am awaiting the minutes to come. I cannot work. So, I am just sitting and waiting for what the future holds!*

The letter ended with his usual signature in Kannada, which was a series of curls representing the words 'Ko. Shi. Karantha'.

Bhat continues his account of those difficult days. 'On the night before Harsha's surgery, Karanth appeared very distressed and pensive. He seemed to have foreseen the prolonged painful agony and eventual tragedy of losing Harsha. Karanth told me, "I can't see anybody suffering, and if something were to happen on the surgical table, I won't feel sorry."

'The major surgery took a few hours. Harsha's lungs had entirely collapsed under a 14-pound tumour that was removed.

'What surprised Karanth was the number of people who came to visit Harsha in the hospital, including the famous film actress Waheeda Rehman. It showed that even during his short stay in Bombay, Harsha had endeared himself to so many people.'

Waheeda Rehman was a student and good friend of Amma's step-brother Ramakrishna Alva's wife Jayalakshmi, who was at that time living in Bombay and helping our family cope with the crisis.

Bhat continues, 'When Harsha's body was to be cremated, Karanth placed flowers on his body and did a namaskara with folded hands. I noticed it. I always used to ask Karanth if I did not understand something he did. The day after Harsha was cremated, I asked him whether the namaskara was an involuntary gesture or he had thought it out. He told me, "I always thought I am a self-made man, quite independent, and, who didn't need anybody's help. But Harsha made me realise that we are all a part of a society and are interdependent. Hence so many people came and helped us. For this enlightenment, I felt grateful to Harsha."'

Harshanna had sobered down during his time in Bombay, shedding his earlier wayward attitude to life (chapter 5). However, this came too late in his short life. Harshanna had been very close to Amma. She was completely broken mentally after his death and devastated by the loss. She never really recovered from it.

I had come to Mysore when I was just nineteen and stayed on there for the next four years, completing my bachelor's degree, and then my master's degree in psychology.

## *Sooryanna, a pillar of strength*

Amma had her first obvious manic episode soon after Harshanna died and had to be brought to Bangalore for psychiatric treatment. I had to accompany her with Tata. We got her treated and took her back to Puttur. After Harshanna's passing away, Amma was clinically diagnosed with manic depressive disorder. Shivaram's friend, Dr Jayaram, was her psychiatrist. Because she was such a warm, extroverted person normally, many people did not recognise her emerging manic episodes.

During those difficult days, my cousin Sooryanarayana was more than a brother to me, and like a son to my parents. He was Tata's younger brother Narasimha Karanth's son. Having lost his own father somewhat early, Soorya became a surrogate son to my parents. Soorya was eight years older than me. From the time he was sixteen years of age, he used to come to Balavana to spend his summer holidays. Soorya was a wonderful human being, although not a very bright student. Even after he finished school and became a physical education instructor at Kota High School, he used to visit us often in Balavana.

Soorya was always very devoted to Amma. She sometimes developed painful cracks on the skin of her heels. Soorya would soak her feet in a bucket of hot water, scrub them and apply petroleum jelly diligently and regularly. He cared for it until all cracks on her heels fully healed.

After Tata moved from Puttur to Saligrama near Kota in 1974, Soorya took much responsibility for my parents' welfare. He served them with devotion until his premature death in 1988 (chapter 10).

To return to my story, after Harshanna's death, Tata's telegrams asking me to rush home to help him manage Amma arrived fairly frequently during my years in Mysore. And they continued to arrive after I moved to Bangalore to do my post graduate diploma at the All India Institute of Mental Health (AIIMH, now NIMHANS).

Amma's manic episodes occurred once every two years. During these episodes, Amma would be totally out of control. Tata could not manage her on his own. He would often summon me to help. Soorya also arrived from Kota to help. Both of us would take Amma to Bangalore and get her treated by the famous psychiatrist, Dr S.S. Jayaram. He was later my teacher when I studied clinical psychology in Bangalore.

After Amma calmed down with medications, we returned home with the drug prescriptions. During her depressive phases and episodes, which lasted for months and years, Amma was listless and dormant. She would sit by herself, looking immensely sad, and not do anything at all.

Due to these psychiatric episodes of Amma, each time I came home, my relationship with her changed. In a way, I became her mother, rather than her being mine. When I was studying psychology in Mysore, I was getting increasingly interested in the subject of mental health. I was eager to learn about the mental illness Amma was suffering from so that I could help her.

Until Ullas and Kshama grew up and started helping with Amma, I had to handle most of her psychiatric episodes on my own. That was a difficult time for our family. But Soorya was ever so helpful. Apart from my parents, to whom I wrote every week, I exchanged numerous letters sharing my sorrows and joys with Soorya.

## My marriage to Ravi

When I joined the diploma program at AIIMH, I met my future husband, Ravinder Lal Kapur, a medical doctor who was a fellow student. Soon after I got a telegram from Tata saying that Amma had been diagnosed with cancer and had to be rushed to Bombay for surgery. I read the telegram and exclaimed, 'My poor father!' Ravi, who was then just a friend, asked me why I was more concerned about my father when it was my mother who had cancer.

I had to explain my remark. Each time Amma had her manic attacks, Tata was devastated. He found the situation very difficult to handle. I was there for him although I was very fond of Amma too. Tata did not like being in hospitals. I knew Amma's cancer meant he had to be in a hospital for her treatment.

It was not that I did not care about Amma's illness. But at that moment Tata's burden seemed greater because he had to take care of her. When Harshanna was dying, Amma had taken on such a burden. I knew Amma was mentally very tough. She had been in the hospital with Harshanna all the time. She could stay with any patient and take care of anybody in pain. On the other hand, Tata would sit just outside the hospital, feeling miserable, and chain-smoking his Charminar cigarettes.

I immediately took leave and rushed home. I had to manage the household and the printing press. Tata took Amma to Bombay for her surgery, which was successful. Amma came back and lived on for two more decades.

Amma would turn very hostile to Tata during her manic episodes. When she was out of control, she would give away cash or even jewellery to total strangers. When she wanted to visit Sathya

Sai Baba of Puttaparthi, Tata would send her in the car. Sai Baba himself once told her to go back and serve her husband.

After Ravi and I took a liking to each other, the first thing I did was to write to Tata, saying, 'I have met someone I like; he is a Punjabi doctor who is my classmate. Can I bring him home to Balavana?' Even before I started going out with Ravi, I wanted my parents' permission. Tata's cryptic telegram in response to me read, 'You may come if you wish.' I went with Ravi to Puttur anyway.

Tata appeared to be unprepared for my ever getting married. When he saw us enter the gate of the large Balavana compound, he abruptly returned to the bathroom from which he had just emerged. He seemed unsure of how to face the moment. On the other hand, Amma greeted us both warmly and was happy to see a handsome young man with her daughter. However, having heard he was a 'Punjabi', Amma had expected a turbaned Sardar with a flowing beard. To Ravi, who was wearing a white kurta and pyjamas, her first question was, 'Are you a Mohammedan?' Amma was so direct and warm.

After that first awkward moment, even Tata got along fine with Ravi. In fact, both my parents were very happy. During the two years when we were engaged before our wedding, Ravi used to visit Balavana often.

Ravi's father, Mohan Lal Kapur, was a well-known doctor in Amritsar who had migrated from Lahore after the traumatic Partition. The family, which was very wealthy, had fled from Pakistan with only the clothes they wore: Ravi, the only son, together with four girls. M.L. Kapur had then rebuilt his life in India and become quite a well-known doctor in Amritsar. Because he was in frail health, the decision was made to solemnise our wedding in Amritsar following the Arya Samaj rites. Even in those days, Punjabi weddings were quite ostentatious. Ravi, however, preferred a registered marriage and a simple wedding ceremony.

Malavika's wedding at Amritsar in 1964: Tata, Amma, Malavika, Ravi, Mohanlal Kapur and Vidyavathi Kapur

Tata had asked Ravi what the customary gift to be sent from the bride's family was. Ravi's mother had suggested that the traditional five almonds be sent as 'shagun' (good omen). In Punjab, that meant five baskets of dry fruits. Tata promptly sent a packet that contained exactly five almond nuts via registered post, leading to much hilarity all round.

Between 1966 and 1970, we went to the University of Edinburgh for Ravi to pursue his doctoral degree. I worked as a psychologist to financially support ourselves. I corresponded with Tata regularly. When we came back from Scotland in 1970, Ravi had a research grant from the University of Edinburgh to work on a project for comparatively studying patterns of mental illnesses among patrilineal castes such as Brahmins and matrilineal ones such as Bunts, Mogaveeras and Billavas.

Because of our family roots in Kota, the project was based there. This study in social psychiatry was later published as *The Great Universe of Kota*, a literal translation of the Kota Brahmin's grandiose title for their homeland.[43] Tata was so fascinated by the book that he took it upon himself to translate it into Kannada, publishing it under literally the same title.[44]

Later, in 1974, when Ravi and I moved to work in Manipal Hospital for a year, we often dropped in at Saligrama where my parents had just moved. Tata was curious about Ravi's professional work, seeking out even minute case details. Ravi admired Tata greatly because he too had a wide range of similar interests, including theatre and music. Ravi also was an ethical atheist like Tata. There was a very warm personal equation between them. Amma, of course, was generally fond of Ravi, although her health was her greatest preoccupation by then.

After my parents moved to Saligrama, Soorya and his wife Sumathi (1939-2021) were pillars of strength to them both (chapter 10). By this time Amma had become not only deeply religious but also turned into a believer of Brahminical rituals formally conducted by priests. Since Tata did not care for these, Soorya would organise the rituals for Amma in the ancestral house in Kota. However, Amma's health continued to decline (chapter 10).

## Amma's death

In 1986, Amma was very sick, semi-conscious and sometimes delirious, even three months before she died. Once, when I was tending to her, she suddenly burst out crying and called out to me. She wept bitterly, saying, 'Ullas has died!' I consoled her, telling her that it was Harsha who had died a long time ago, and Ullas was very much alive. Then she felt better and resumed her singing.

Amma was in and out of Manipal Hospital much of the time. Tata finally decided to bring her home when the medical treatments were proving futile. Even the day before she died, doctors had

---

43   See B-31 in Annotated Bibliography for more details
44   See B-32 in Annotated Bibliography for more details

suggested hospitalisation. Tata said, 'I don't want her to be a piece of meat on a table, to be poked and probed and kept alive like that. I want her to die at home.'

She passed away the next day—23 September 1986. I was at her side, but Ullas and Tata had gone to Manipal to consult doctors.

We decided to cremate Amma's body the next day. That night, clouds gathered and heavy rain looked imminent. Tata was worried about the proper conduct of the cremation, just in case it rained. He kept asking Soorya nervously, 'What should we do, Soorya, if it rains?' As usual, Soorya was quite the pillar of strength to all of us. He assured Tata that a 'chappara' (shelter made of bamboo and palm fronds) could be erected quickly to enable proper cremation. However, the next morning, the skies cleared and the sun shone brightly.

Truth be told, when Amma passed away, it was a great relief for everybody. Seeing her once vibrant persona in this miserable condition had been an awful experience for all of us and we accepted that it was time for her to go in peace.

When Amma was being cremated, bus-loads of people from the neighbourhood came to pay their respects. Strangers touched her feet and sought her blessings. She was dressed as a 'sumangali'. As Tata had wished, her body was decked in the marigold flowers that she loved. People kept commenting that 'Leelamma looks like a Devi'. Amma had always said she wanted to die a sumangali, not as a widow. She had her wish.

A couple of years later, in 1988, at Bangalore, I got a phone call that stunned me. Soorya had died in a motor accident. I immediately rushed to Saligrama, and went up to Tata's study. As I walked in, Tata looked up, sobbing. He said, '*Soorya innu illa.*' (Soorya is no longer with us.) This was the first and last time I ever saw Tata cry. To him, losing Soorya was more than losing his own son. For him, Soorya had been an anchor. No one could fill that role, including his own children.

## *Tata and his grandchildren*

Tata with his children and grandchildren: Seated– Padmanabha Rau (Babu), Kshama, Tata, Malavika and Ullas. Standing– Krithi, Kavya, Nishanth

Tata loved his grandchildren. My son Sharad and daughter Svapna used to spend their summer holidays with him. Kshama's daughter Kavya and son Nishanth spent even more time with Tata (chapter 9). Ullas's daughter Krithi, his youngest grandchild, also visited him. They all loved him. It was a special thrill because they all enjoyed the same treats from him that we had enjoyed as children: endless stories, dolls, masks and travel.

My daughter Svapna was his first granddaughter. For that reason, and because she was studious, she was his favourite grandchild. The two boys, Sharad and Nishanth, were very naughty and often got on his nerves. Tata was then in his seventies, living alone, and at times got angry with the boys. All the grandchildren have very fond memories of Tata.

Svapna studied medicine in Manipal and married her fellow student Sameer Sabnis. While we lived in Bangalore, their simple wedding was celebrated in our home in Koramangala, which I had named 'Balavana'. Soorya had played the role of her eldest maternal uncle in that Arya Samaj-style wedding ritual.

Below are some memories of Tata in Svapna's own words:

I feel so fortunate that I was able to have a close relationship with my grandfather, Shivarama Karanth (I called him Tata as well!) both as a child and into my early adulthood.

My oldest memories go back to his Balavana home. I must have been around four or five years old. I remember roaming those wooded acres and the home at the top of a little hillock. Further up the hill was his printing press, which was still in use when I was little. I found it to be a fascinating, noisy and busy place. I also remember playing and climbing trees with other children from the neighbourhood.

I was a voracious reader from a young age and would sit upstairs reading, keeping Tata company while he worked. I was quiet and did not bother him. Every night he told me stories. I would supply the character or situation and he would take it from there. If I wanted fairies, horses or a child who learned to fly, that story would be instantly born. How I wish I had written those down or taped the dozens of stories he spun for me.

Sometimes, when he was at his desk, he would look over at me, and call me, 'Magu (child), come here.' He would pick up a pair of scissors, fold some paper or cardboard to draw a little sketch. He would then cut, shape and staple the paper. In minutes I would have an articulated paper tiger with moving legs. It was magic.

Tata once made me a beautiful set of wings out of wire, fabric and crepe paper that I played with until they fell apart. He would give me his expensive pens that no other adult would let me use. He knew I was careful and would return them to him unscathed. Tata was not a demonstrative person, but this was how he showed his love. Even as a small child I could feel his warmth, even though I cannot remember him ever actually hugging me.

Tata enjoyed my company, as I did his.

Svapna switches her narrative, talking about Amma:

I have good memories of my grandmother too, from Balavana. I also called her Amma.

She answered my incessant questions, treating each with respect, and never being condescending, as many adults were. Once I demanded that I wanted my ears pierced. Amma took me to the goldsmith in Puttur town and got it done. She even gifted me a lovely pair of little gold ear studs, much to my parents' consternation later.

Tata and Amma moved to Saligrama when we were away in Scotland for a year. When we returned, we were in Manipal for a year and then moved to Bangalore. My younger brother Sharad and my other cousins used to spend the vacations at Saligrama with Tata and Amma. During my teens, I did not spend much time with them. But when I joined the medical school in Manipal, my fiancé, Samir, and I visited Saligrama regularly. Tata loved our visits.

He had a smallish study, packed with books. There was the entire time-life series of books on mythology, beautiful books on various artists, books on science and history. He would read these books, and when he ran out of shelf space, he would donate them to a nearby school or library. I insisted that when he was ready to give away his art books, they should come to me, and he kept his word, and I have them to this day.

After medical college, my husband Samir and I moved to the United States (US) for residency training. Once we came back to Bangalore, we visited Tata in Saligrama, which was just wonderful. I don't remember what we talked about, but I had a premonition that this would be my last meeting with him. He was in his mid-90s, after all. The next morning, as we got ready to leave, Tata asked me to pick some memento from the showcase. There were statues and medals and different ornaments. I chose a beautiful picture of Tata, standing against a bunch of saplings. His dhoti was snow white against the lush green plants. I still have it in my living room.

On 9 December 1997, my mother called me in the US to tell me Tata had passed away. My son was born a year after Tata died. Had Tata lived only one more year he could have seen his first great-grandson.

## Final memories of Tata

When Tata suffered a stroke on 4 December 1997, I dashed from Bangalore in a taxi with Ullas to the hospital in Manipal. Doctors had put him on a ventilator. After four days without any sign of recovery, all three of us wanted him taken off the ventilator. We were sure he would not have agreed to be on such life support if he were aware of his condition.

However, the doctors had a problem: 'If we don't do whatever is possible to keep Shivarama Karanth alive, the public will feel we didn't take care of him.'

We, as his children, could not change this situation, because there was no provision in Indian law for rational euthanasia. Mercifully, Tata died of acidosis on 9 December, and the ventilator had to come off.

I recall how much we had all rejoiced when Tata had received the prestigious Jnanpith Award in 1977. At that time, Tata had asked me what I wanted as a memento from him. I had asked him for a second-hand 'tamboori', which he had got from his musician friend, Vasudeva Nayak of Kundapur.

Some years later, Tata gifted me a part of his Jnanpith Award, the beautiful bronze statuette of Vagdevi, the goddess of learning. At the same time, he gifted the original award citation document to Ullas. He had split the award between his two older children. When the museum in Balavana was being established as a memorial to Tata by the Karnataka government, the deputy commissioner of South Kanara requested us for some important memorabilia belonging to Tata for the display. I gifted my most precious possession, that bronze icon of Vagdevi, without a second thought. Ullas did likewise with his citation script. I truly believe Tata was a national treasure and it was my duty to share his memory with the public at large. There are other gifts from Tata that I still cherish.

Travelling and being by myself are things I enjoy. Not many women in our society like to travel alone. I am often teased by my friends that I too have wheels on my feet, just like Tata.

Tata had travelled all over India in his youth. He had very little money. His staple diet in those days was Bengal gram soaked in water. Very few Kannada writers had such intense wanderlust. I know why he did it. Sometimes I also pick up my rucksack and go trekking, solely in anticipation of that exhilaration.

I sometimes envy Tata. He had seen the giant Buddha statues in Bamiyan, Afghanistan before those magnificent sculptures were destroyed by Taliban bigots. I have travelled to Africa, even been to Timbuctoo. I am sure Tata would have loved to hear from me about that trip.

I still travel a lot both for professional reasons and leisure. Unlike most professors who make their students collect the basic survey data, I do that myself. I should be able to directly work with village children if I am to write about my work. Tata also based his novels on his authentic, hands-on experiences. He had a photographic memory. Wherever Tata went in Karnataka, he would know his way around in detail. Unfortunately, he did not pass on that capability to me.

In my career, I have tried to follow Tata's ideas about children's education. I dream that all these tribal children I work with should have access to the kind of education I got from Tata and Amma in Balavana. These are ideas related to the 'child-centred play-way method'. In 2007, I published a book titled, *Learning from Children, What to Teach Them*. When I give my talks, I often find myself echoing a lot of Tata's beliefs. He had once said, 'Schools are slaughterhouses of children's inborn curiosity.'

People sometimes ask me, 'It is said that nothing grows under the shade of a banyan tree. Was your father not a banyan tree?' I respond by saying, 'No, Tata was like a kalpavriksha (coconut palm), which generously gave away every bit of itself to others. He did not stunt our growth like a banyan tree. Because he allowed us to chart the course of our own lives and follow our true passions, we have all thrived.'

Tata was not our personal possession. We were glad to share him with the whole wide world.

# 5

# A BOY'S WORLD

*K. Ullas Karanth*

The Karanth family in Balavana in the early 1950s: Tata,
Ullas, Kshama, Amma, Malavika and Harshanna

### *A boy grows up in Balavana*

My earliest memories are from three years of age. Tata was not
demonstratively affectionate with me like he truly was with Kshama.
I did not particularly worry about this. I was happy to avoid him
as I went about my own lazy, freewheeling way. As boys go, I was
the sloppy, undisciplined, dreamy type rather than one of those
suicidally mischievous types.

Tata was a friend of the then dharmadharshi (guiding trustee) of the famed Dharmasthala temple, Manjayya Heggade (1889-1955), who was reputed for his piety and fairness. A great big festival called Nadaavali is held irregularly, once a few decades, in Dharmasthala. Thousands of devotees congregate and many religious rituals and cultural events are celebrated. One afternoon, during the Nadaavali of 1951, while Tata and Amma were deeply engaged in conversation with Heggade in his mansion, I sneaked away and soon got lost in the massive crowd outside.

There was utter panic in the household, with announcements being made on loudspeakers about a lost three-year-old boy. I did not, in fact, realise I was 'lost'. I was fascinated by some men seated in a row, impressively attired in khaki uniform, wearing tall tubular red turbans and khaki wraparound socks. I went up to them to chat. Policemen in Kanara those days were invariably burly men over six feet tall, nothing like their bonsai versions we see around us now. As I kept them regaled, loudspeakers blared messages about the missing three-year-old boy. One of the policemen picked me up and dashed up to Heggade's mansion, ending the boy-hunt. For some reason, I still remember that row of policemen in that impressive attire vividly.

As I grew up, Tata phenomenally enriched my mind through stories he read out from the illustrated books in his wonderful library, or the fantastic tales he spun off on the spur of the moment at bedtime. Despite these wonderful exchanges, I feared Tata because of his violent temper, which I saw him lose quite often.

A typical example was that of the religious mendicant, Basavayya, who towed around a 'nandi' (sacred bull) in the streets of Puttur, playing a loud, harsh tune on his 'walaga' (pipe-like wind instrument). For some reason, during his weekly rounds, Basavayya chose to visit Balavana around noon, exactly the time Tata took his precious power nap. If Amma did not stop Basavayya's horrible dirge quickly by paying him off, I was guaranteed an exciting spectacle.

An extremely angry Tata would rush down the spiral staircase, loudly cursing the mendicant. Tata would dash to the culm of the yellow *Vulgaris* bamboo in our front yard. He would try to break off a twig with the intention of whipping the guardian of the sacred bull. The fibrous bamboo twig would not yield, and after a few futile tugs at it, as the offending music stopped, Tata's temper would cool down. He then went up the spiral stairs silently, looking somewhat sheepish. I tittered with great joy mocking the chastened Basavayya.

I was sure I did not want to face Tata's wrath, though.

When I did something mischievous, Tata would get angry and threaten to thrash me. He rarely did, because his raised voice and angry countenance were sufficient to cow me down. I recall one instance, however, when I messed up his work table by overturning an ink pot and escaped stealthily to hide in the bathroom. When Tata returned home, he whacked me on my butt so hard that I peed in my shorts. Tata then suddenly felt regretful and quickly pacified me.

Tata had pioneered the introduction of the gentle Montessori training methods for his experimental school at Balavana. He genuinely loved horsing around entertaining children. For a whole generation of Kannada children, he was 'Karanthajja' (grandfather Karanth) through his popular weekly column in *Taranga* magazine. I am sure none of those children he enthralled will believe my tales.

Despite his great admiration for the gentle Maria Montessori and the pacifist Mahatma Gandhi, Tata firmly believed in corporal punishment as a tool to discipline children, and, for that matter, adults too.

## *Amma*

All three of us have written with much feeling about Amma in this book. There are also some other fine articles about her that show what a talented, capable, warm-hearted person she was.[45]

All that was before the manic-depressive psychiatric traits kicked in and dominated Amma's personality. Some of her warmth always remained, but her extraordinary abilities and talent had withered away by the time she was in her forties. Because I was just twelve

---

45   See B-22, B-23 and B-27 in Annotated Bibliography for more details

when her serious decline began, I saw only the twilight of her extraordinary persona. In the last quarter-century of her life, she became a pale shadow of the feisty Leela Alva who had married Tata at just seventeen years of age and become the central pillar of his life. For the next quarter-century, the entire architecture of Tata's creative life was built around that pillar.

Tata had married Amma in a civil ceremony on 6 May 1936 in Mangalore. The news of their inter-caste wedding had caused much social consternation among orthodox Brahmins as well as Bunts. One of Amma's maternal uncles from her Kadenja Guthu clan was so overwrought that he allegedly slapped his forehead in despair and cried out, *'che, che, che, yenna kulaku onji aibu!'* (What a blot on my clan!). There was also a Brahmin journalist in Udupi, aghast at this 'varna sankara' (racial or inter-caste mixing), who wrote defamatory articles in his tabloid. Tata, feisty as ever, successfully sued the journalist for libel. That aggressive champion of orthodoxy also stuck to his principles and chose to go to jail rather than plead guilty and pay a fine.

Years later, I once asked Amma how she felt walking down the street with Tata in such a stressful milieu. She said she sometimes overheard people snidely whispering, 'Look, there comes Shivarama *Shetty'* in Tulu. I was curious what Tata's response was. Amma said, 'Your Tata is so immersed in his own thoughts, none of this ever registered in his mind. As for myself, I was quite okay if they labelled him a Bunt.'

### Amma's kin in Balavana

Amma set up home with Tata in Balavana in 1936. After Kamu Alva died in 1937, Tata agreed to shelter Amma's younger sisters—Rathna, Ahalya and Sarojini, who were being ill-treated by their stepmother. Tata took the initiative to get all of Amma's sisters married, including her elder sister Savithri, who was staying with her uncle Gopala Alva.

Savithri Alva (1918-2005) was married to Tata's friend and

staunch Gandhian Kochanna Bhandari (1907-1953). He had moved to Assam in 1932 to provide relief to the victims of the great earthquake, under the advice of his mentor, Thakkar Bapa, the well-known Gandhian. Kochanna Bhandari settled in Assam, established an ashram and was eventually recognised as a great social worker.[46] A statue commemorating Bhandari stands in Guwahati to this day. That is how I have several first cousins, all married to Assamese spouses: although Bunts by birth, they are proudly Assamese in every way. They speak neither Tulu nor Kannada.

Tata got Amma's younger sister Ahalya Alva (1927-86), who he was very fond of, married to his good friend, writer and publisher Sheshagiri Rao Kulkarni of Dharwad. 'Ahalya Chikkamma', as we called her, was a beauty. She was a talented writer who made a name for herself in Kannada literature as Geetha Kulkarni.

Amma's two other sisters, Rathna and Sarojini, were also married, respectively, to Manjayya Shetty and Manjappa Bhandari. They visited Balavana rarely and our contact with them was sporadic.

Although Amma disliked her stepmother, Pushpavathi, she was very fond of her step-brother, Ramakrishna Alva (1931-85). He did not like his mother, who apparently ill-treated him also. He also 'ran away' to Bombay, became a dancer and married out of the community to Jayalakshmi who also became a well-known Bharatanatyam teacher in Bombay and then in Mangalore. Their daughter Araty Shetty (née Alva) still connects with us and was of great help to me in researching Amma's family history for this book.

Although our homelife in Balavana was not traditionally Brahminical, our dietary customs were. When Amma had set up home in Balavana, a Bunt landlord in our neighborhood was concerned about her diet. He earnestly offered to secretly smuggle some Bunt-style chicken curry from time to time for Amma! He was surprised to hear Amma had given up eating meat, well before she had married Tata.

---

46   See B-33 in Annotated Bibliography for more details

However, following the South Kanara tradition, two kinds of rice were cooked at our home at mealtime. Amma, Harshanna and I ate the boiled brown rice that the non-Brahmins preferred, whereas Tata and my two sisters liked the polished white rice which the Brahmins ate.

Amma's younger cousin, Tyampanna Chowta of Kadenja, was an occasional visitor to Balavana. He was a well-off merchant, a jovial man who regaled us with his funny stories. Chowta was keen that Amma and her sisters should legally fight for their share of properties in Kadenja Guthu, which were in adverse possession of some relatives. However, Amma decided not to go through the necessary protracted litigation, despite his offer to assist.

Chowta's sons turned out to be enterprising young men who established successful photographic laboratories and other businesses in Bombay, Mysore and Mangalore.

Amma's grandmother, Akkamma, who everyone called Mallappe (the great mother) came to live with us in Balavana in 1958. A talented lady, Mallappe could sing Tulu folk songs, Kannada Yakshagana songs and bhajans in Hindi.

Amma's grandmother, Akkamma (Mallappe), was a talented singer. She stayed with us in Balavana in the 1950s before her death at age 96.

However, by the time I saw her, she was in her mid-90s, quite senile, and thus a great source of amusement to me. She used to refer to Tata in Tulu as 'upadeshilu' (protestant preacher) because of his shoulder-length hair. Mallappe's rendition of Ramayana in Tulu was truly hilarious. In her version, when Rama and Sita reach their destination to commence vanavasa, they find no forest there at all. Because, as Mallappe explained, 'All the trees had been chopped down and carted away by greedy Konkani timber merchants.' Kshama and I took great delight in teasing her, often provoking Amma to step in and discipline us.

Mallappe's son from her first husband was Mundappa Poonja, a tall, dark man who sported a silvery-white handlebar moustache. He was a retired police constable who lived near Manjeshwara. He came to Balavana, invariably in the mango-fruiting season, to visit his mother and took back a big basket of mangoes. Poonja barely spoke to Tata, but persistently pestered Amma for small loans.

Amma used to address her uncle Poonja as 'Munda Pappa'. Tata, the every-ready punster, used to joke those mangoes that Mundappa took were also of the Mundappa variety, but if over-ripe, they too could be called 'Munda-Pappa'.

Amma's uncle, Gopala Alva, had moved back from Bombay to Mangalore in 1930 with his elder brother Kamu Alva. He was a friend of V.R. Mirajkar, a Mangalorean who made his fortune as a surgeon in Lahore. Gopala Alva had supervised the construction of a gigantic mansion for his friend in Mangalore. That magnificent building, which Mirajkar donated to the government, now houses the official Museum of Mangalore in Bijai. It bears Mirajkar's mother Srimanthi Bai's name.

Gopala Alva was a complex man. He was a devotee of Swami Vivekananda. He never got married but did have a consort named Kalyani who also moved to Puttur with him. Gopala Alva was an avid punter, visiting Bangalore once a year to gamble at the horse races. His rather creative explanation for his non-saintly hobby was that in case god brought him luck, he would apply the winnings at the track to build an orphanage for destitute children.

Gopala Alva and Tata were on very good terms. When Tata left on his two-month trip to Europe in the 1950s, Alva moved to Balavana to manage Tata's printing press. Tata had borrowed the money needed to cover his Europe trip from his friend Manjanathaiah (chapter 6).

Sometime after his return, when Alva jocularly asked Tata if he felt like he had visited 'swarga loka' (heaven), Tata's pungent riposte was, 'Indeed. It did for a while, but now my debt burden makes me feel like going to "pathala loka" (deep underground).' Although Tata did not realise it, Alva took this barb to heart. After a few days, he simply disappeared and was never seen again. Although we heard rumours that he had become a sanyasi in Kashi, I do not lend credence to these rumours, because there is no race track in that holy city.

Mallappe died after Gopala Alva disappeared. She was ninety-six.

The sleepless nights imposed on Amma, as she tended to Mallappe's needs, and the stress of managing Balavana during the financial crunch took a heavy toll on Amma's health. A few days after Mallappe died, I witnessed Amma's mental breakdown for the first time. I was deeply disturbed and wanted my old Amma back. That Leela Karanth, however, was gone forever.

## *Explorations with Tata*

I think the love for animals is hardwired in some of us. Tata and his younger brother Narasimha Karanth were two such men. I, too, have inherited that trait. Tata had even established a menagerie in Balavana in the 1930s. It exhibited large animals like the sambar, chital and blackbuck. When Amma was alone in Balavana once, a chital stag escaped from its holding stockade. She watched helplessly as her two huge German Shepherd dogs, disobeying her command, attacked and killed the stag.

During the Second World War, when food was severely rationed, Amma had to plead with the assistant commissioner in Puttur, Thimmappa Shetty, for extra rations for these German Shepherds.

She believed he granted her request only because she, too, was a Bunt like him. Incidentally, that benevolent officer's grandson, Salil Shetty, later became the head of Amnesty International.

By the time I grew up, Tata had closed down the menagerie in Balavana. However, there were always dogs, of one kind or the other, ranging from pure-bred German Shepherds to various crossbreeds. All of them were compelled to be vegetarians like us.

Tata read aloud the tiger-hunter Jim Corbett's *Man-eaters of Kumaon* to me. He also consistently encouraged me to pursue my inborn interest in natural history. By home-schooling me for five years, Tata gave me the opportunity to wander around Balavana, identifying birds. He was very pleased when, by the age of eight, I had become a proficient bird watcher under the guidance of family friend Vasantha Sathyashankar (née Mundkur).

In my pre-teen years, once or twice a year, Tata would take me (and Kshama) on week-long car trips across wide swathes of Karnataka. Along the way he would attend literary functions, participate in meetings and do some sightseeing, always staying at the home of one or the other of his friends. Tata had given up driving in the 1940s, soon after he learned to. I am sure it was a wise decision that saved many lives. For the long road trips, he hired a taxi until he could afford a car and a driver in 1960.

During these field trips, I would listen, wonderstruck, as Tata expounded with great erudition on everything that we saw along the way: the geology, landscapes, forests, wildlife, agriculture, archaeology, temples, monuments, culture, folk art, customs, rituals and generally about the Kannada land and its people. I paid close attention, trying to absorb as much as I could. Even to this day, I find the breadth of Tata's general knowledge in so many domains quite astounding. I have never met anyone, anywhere in the world, any time, who possessed a similar breadth of knowledge. Tata truly bridged the two cultures, of the sciences and the arts, that the great English novelist C.P. Snow had recognised.

Tata had only a high school diploma to his credit. However, as the years passed, he received several honorary doctorates from many universities.

Although I grew up in Puttur in the southern part of South Kanara, once or twice a year, we visited Tata's ancestral home in Kota, in the north. These two cultures were very different. In the south, Tulu was the lingua franca, whereas to the north of the Seethanadi river, people spoke the Kundapura dialect of Kannada. Tata had grown up speaking that dialect, but never used it except in phrases or sentences in his novels. Tata had never learned to speak Tulu, although he could understand it.

In those days, the journey from Puttur to Kota, 130 kilometres which now takes a little over two hours, took an entire day. Two major west-flowing rivers at Kallianpur and Mabukala were not yet bridged. Our car was ferried on two conjoined boats with a wooden platform tied up on top. These ferry boats were locally called 'jungles'.

At Kota, we stayed with Tata's younger brother Narasimha Karanth who had inherited the ancestral house as his share of Shesha Karanth's properties. He excelled at catching snakes and keeping smaller wild animals as pets. His second son, Sooryanarayana, became deeply bonded to our family and was like a sibling to all of us.

During one of those visits to Kota, I witnessed for the first time a traditional Yakshagana Bayalata. It was an all-night performance in the dim, magical light of palmyra torches. This was before kerosene gas lights and later electricity, made their jarring impact on that fine art form. The Bayalata was a stunning spectacle. The charismatic artiste Haradi Rama Ganiga had played the role of warrior Arjuna.

I also associate these visits to Kota with meeting my uncle, K.L. Karanth, who lived in Kundapura. He was a science teacher, horticulturist and philanthropist of repute. He was a stern person and a rationalist like Tata. My uncle was a hardworking, muscular man whose daily exercise routine was to chop firewood. I once requested him to turn on the radio to listen to cricket commentary. He instantly retorted that a growing boy like me should be outdoors playing cricket, and not listening to rubbish on the radio. He compared the real joy of playing cricket to the pleasure of eating holiges, and the cricket commentary to listening to some stranger *describing* someone else eating holiges! What is the fun in that, he asked. He had me stumped!

Another family from Kota with close ties to the Karanths through complex networks of intermarriages over generations, were the Hollas of 'Upparige Mane' (The Storied House) in Kota. The Hollas were pioneers of the Udupi restaurant business model that took roots in Bangalore in the early twentieth century. They were contemporaries of the more famous Mayya family, also from Kota, who established the global brand of MTR vegetarian cuisine.

The patriarch of the Holla family was Anandarama Holla (1928-2021). He was a charismatic, socially prominent man of Bangalore. Anandarama Holla was a domineering personality. He was devoted to Tata, and once proudly told me he was Tata's 'shishya'. In 1971, Anandarama Holla took the entire responsibility for organising Kshama's wedding impeccably, at the headquarters of the Kota Brahmin Association's kalyana mantapa (marriage hall) in Bangalore.

Tata's relative Anandarama Holla of Upparige Mane in Kota was
a prominent hotelier in Bangalore. He hosted us during visits to Bangalore
for many years and supported Tata in very many ways.

When visiting Bangalore with Tata, we used to stay in the cavernous, huge joint family house of the Hollas, which was built annexed to their well-known Udupi Krishna Bhavan restaurant in one of the labyrinthine lanes of Balepet. These visits to the Holla home were great fun. The miracle was, you could tap on a small porthole that connected the house to the restaurant, and order whatever delicacy you fancied. Minutes later, a man's hand would stretch out of the porthole to deliver the order: delicious dosas, idlis, jalebis and jamuns, whatever ... It was heaven on earth.

Another cousin of mine in Bangalore who supported Tata over the years was K.R. Dayananda Karanth (1930-94) who inherited his father K.R. Karanth's legal practice. Tata fought many legal battles in the Karnataka High Court with Dayananda leading the charge, always pro bono, of course, until his tragic death in a car accident. His son, Sachindra, is the third generation of Karanths continuing K.R. Karanth's law practice, while also being the informal archivist of the Karanth clan.

## *Balavana: where east met west*

Balavana was a six-acre wooded lot about three kilometres away from Puttur town. Our house was built in two parts. The older structure with a tiled roof, which Tata had built in the early 1930s, housed the kitchen, the store, a large dining room and two bedrooms, with a large jagali. The second block, which Tata designed and built in 1938, was in an elegant western style. It had a spiral staircase entirely cast in concrete, a rarity in those days. It had two levels, with the lower one having a large, common 'sleeping room', with an adjacent room used to store books and paper stock. The same plan was duplicated upstairs, with the larger room serving as Tata's office and library and the adjacent room reserved for his post-lunch power nap. Both rooms had wall-to-wall bookshelves.

Balavana had modern amenities rare in India's rural homes of those days. In the 1940s itself, Tata had installed a diesel generator to provide electric power, long before Puttur town got its public utility supply. If I remember right, the very first of these power generators ran not on diesel fuel, but on crude oil.

In the early 1950s, Tata owned a used Hillman car of 1940s vintage. I recall being in it when it crashed into a bus. Although unhurt, I remember crying merely looking at the wreckage. Tata could not afford a car for a decade after that. He purchased a used Standard Vanguard car in 1960, which pleased me mightily.

Tata was a fastidious man who bathed twice a day. At home, we had a toilet with ceramic 'Asian pans' connected to a septic tank, one among only a dozen or so homes in Puttur that sported such a convenience. The primitive practice of manual scavenging was the norm for most homes in the town, whereas the rural folk simply headed to the bushes in times of need.

## Boiled eggs in Balavana

Despite India's rather recent colonial history, in the 1950s westerners were a rare sight in Kanara. However, because of Tata's accomplishments in domains beyond Kannada literature, he had gained a wider name recognition beyond India. As a result, occasionally, foreigners visited him and stayed in Balavana. Tata made just one culinary concession for them: in addition to our routine vegetarian fare, they got boiled eggs.

Some of these visitors left a deep impression on my young mind.

The anthropologist Christopher Von Fuerer Haimendorf (1909-1995) was known for his work on the tribes of India. He and his wife Betty stayed with us in 1953. Tata took them to the great cardamom forest estate, 'Neriya Male', to acquaint Haimendorf with the Male Kudiya tribal people who lived there. Although I was only five when we hosted the Haimendorfs, I was very touched when the old couple made it a point to track me down in Mysore, while on a trip to India in the 1980s.

In 1958, Bengt Hager of the International Archives of Sweden came down to Puttur to present Tata with a medal in recognition of his monumental work on the Yakshagana folk art. This prestigious international recognition spread Tata's reputation widely across India's cultural circles.

Kshama and I were fascinated by a lady visitor named Susie, who was a part of a UNESCO team that worked with Tata on an adult literacy project. Susie was the first African-American person we had ever seen. We followed her around like puppies. Amused by us, she gifted us a mechanical toy mouse that ran and tumbled when wound up, much to our delight.

Another early foreign visitor to Balavana was an Austrian graduate student of anthropology, Luisa Kolinhaufer, who came to study the Bunt community of Kanara. Tata's scholarly Bunt friend, Agrala Purandara Rai, assisted her in her fieldwork.

In the late 1960s, a doctoral student from the University of Michigan, Martha Ashton, came to study Yakshagana under Tata's guidance. She kept contact with our family for years after that. She later had a disagreement with Tata over his experimental version of Yakshagana that successfully took the art form beyond the limits of Karnataka.

Another visitor was a French student of Advaita philosophy, Paul Martin Dubost. Tata had set up visits to various Advaita mathas through his friend Srinivasa Jois, who lived in the village of Hariharapura, in Chikmagalur district. Dubost had a problem finding his destination. A true Frenchman, he could pronounce neither the consonant 'ha' nor 'ra'. When he sought directions to the village 'AaYee-AaAa-PuA', which is how he pronounced Hariharapura, he confounded everyone he asked.

When these westerners stayed in Balavana, my school friends were full of questions about them that only I could answer with authority: such as, did they not wash their backsides? Indeed true: because along with boiled eggs, toilet rolls also arrived in Balavana preceding their visits.

### My brother, Harshanna

My eldest sibling, Harsha, was born on 6 February 1938. He had a rocky relationship with Tata right from his boyhood. Amma, however, pampered him as the first-born son. Unlike Malakka, who was very studious and disciplined, Harshanna was a 'tough guy' who collected many loutish friends who sponged off him.

After his matriculation in Puttur, Harshanna was sent to MGM College, Udupi. However, he escaped from the classes to revel in the company of a friend named Chella Pillai, who was an avid hunter. Harshanna once proudly showed me a photo of a leopard they had killed in the scrub forests, where the campus of Manipal University stands today.

After Harshanna failed his college examinations, Tata ordered him back to Puttur to help run the printing press, Harsha Printery. Tata also set up for him an electrical component store named Harsha Electricals and a franchise of the Bata Shoe Company in Puttur town.

My brother immediately set about bankrupting all these ventures quickly through his profligacy and waywardness. He had many fair weather friends, whom he entertained in great style and at great expense.

I, too, was once a beneficiary of this bonanza when Harshanna hired a van to take his friends to Mangalore to watch a Greco-Roman style 'professional' wrestling show: this was an early version of the World Wrestling Federation type of fakery we now see on television. Harshanna allowed me to tag along to witness Dara Singh (who later became a Bollywood actor) wrestle and 'defeat' King Kong. The glamour of these highly theatrical bouts involving giant foreign wrestlers, staged in a brightly flood-lit arena, could never be matched by the robust and genuine bouts that local wrestlers fought hard and honestly on piles of red earth in broad daylight.

Harshanna also went on to buy a huge Buick limousine of 1930s vintage, once owned by the Maharaja of Baroda, which had seen better days. It had royal seals imprinted on its doors to prove its pedigree.

For all the generosity he showered on his human friends, Harshanna exhibited a deep streak of cruelty towards animals. I recall being absolutely horrified when riding with him in that Buick limousine—he deliberately accelerated to hit a street dog.

Back in Puttur, Harshanna also resumed his hunting trips with his local friends. This was in the 1950s, two decades before India's anti-hunting laws were enacted. However, I was already keen on wild animal protection and hated the idea that my brother was complicit in the slaughter of the last wild animals that still survived in the tropical jungles of Kanara.

When Harshanna did not return home for a couple of days from one such hunting trip, Tata and Amma were worried sick. They feared he may have died, or even been killed in a hunting accident. When he turned up after three days, Tata confronted him angrily but soon broke down. I was deeply disturbed to see the strong man I so feared reduced to tears.

Amma, of course, was always forgiving of Harshanna's transgressions.

In a short time, unsurprisingly, Harshanna's businesses went bankrupt. Tata had to lose his hard-earned money to pay off all his debts. Those were bad days for Tata: I remember him reprimanding poor Amma when she asked him for two rupees for some household expense.

In 1959, Harshanna was packed off to Bombay to earn his living and get trained in the automotive spare parts business under the mentorship of Tata's friend, Moodbidre Sanjiva Rao (chapter 6). The plan was for Harshanna to eventually return to Puttur and set up an automobile workshop. However, Harshanna fell victim to a malignant tumour and died on 30 January 1961.

Living frugally on a small salary in a tenement in Bombay, Harshanna had apparently mellowed down. Many years later, when Malakka showed me a heartfelt letter he had written her from the hospital bed, it moved me to tears, catching myself by surprise. Malakka and he had grown up together and were very fond of each other, although their personalities were as different as chalk and cheese. However, the affection I feel for my two sisters, I never felt for Harshanna.

## *Education at home and in school*

My homeschooling between the ages of six and eleven covered only two subjects, Kannada and Mathematics.

What really opened my eyes to the whole world was a Kannada magazine called *Kasturi*, modelled after *Reader's Digest*. This monthly magazine offered a collection of original as well as translated articles from across the world. The editor of *Kasturi* was a doyen of Kannada journalism, Padigaru Venkataramana Acharya, whose pen names included 'Langulacharya' (literally meaning a teacher with a hairy tail). He was a widely read man with eclectic tastes and had assembled many bright writers who translated articles on a wide range of topics. *Kasturi* cracked open the window to the wider world for me and turned me into a lifelong voracious reader.

I absolutely loved Tata's incredible library with many shelves packed with books. Stacked in there were encyclopedias, including the complete Britannica series. There were all sorts of books on nature, science and the arts, though not much by way of literature.

Displayed in Tata's library were some remarkable paintings. Two of them were original paintings gifted by his friend, the famous artist K.K. Hebbar. There was a large oil painting of Rabindranath Tagore and other paintings of the Shantiniketan School of Art. There were also two works of Tata's friend, the famous Russian artist Magda Nauchman (1889-1951). One was a delicately drawn watercolour portrait of Tata as a handsome young man in his thirties. The other one was a large oil on canvas painting, 'Diana the Huntress'—a stark naked Diana and a female companion, walking two leopards (one spotted and the other black) on leashes.

Tata subscribed to a wide range of English-language magazines: *Reader's Digest, Coronet, National Geographic, Life* and *Time*. However, I could only marvel at the wonderful pictures in them until I started to learn English in high school at the age of eleven.

Although Tata had an extensive collection of western books on natural history, his knowledge of native wild animal species of India was patchy. An instance was when we came across a pair of reddish, dog-like animals with bushy tails sleeping on the road in Devimane Ghat near Sirsi. They scurried away at the sight of our car. Tata told me they were red foxes, pictures of which these animals did resemble. Years later, I realised the animals we had seen were, in fact, dholes (Asiatic wild dogs). Red foxes, in fact, are not found in southern India.

I constantly quizzed Tata about his personal experiences with wildlife. He mentioned the sighting of a wild tiger while hiking down the Kodachadri peak in the Western Ghats in his youth. He also mentioned sighting a pair of black leopards from a bus, while travelling at night in a forest near Shiradi, not far from Puttur. The last large animal in Tata's menagerie in Balavana was a blackbuck, which was killed by a black leopard that broke into its pen.

However, all over India, wildlife was being pushed to the brink of extinction with rampant hunting, logging and forest clearance for farming, after India attained independence. Therefore, in the early 1960s, wildlife sightings were rare. We had packs of jackals invading the orchard in Balavana. I loved to hear their weird chorus of howls at night. Even though rarely, I heard the even more weird 'braying' of the striped hyena that came to hunt feral dogs.

As I absorbed natural history knowledge from specialised books and field visits, I started noticing this disconnect between Tata's broad interest in nature and his lack of awareness about the serious problem of wildlife around us being wiped out by hunters. When Tata published his science encyclopedia, *Vijanana Prapancha*, in the mid-1960s, I recall passionately arguing with him about his averment that wild tigers were so numerous in Malenad that local hunters could never extirpate them. I told him that if a famous writer like him said this in print, his many admirers among the local landed gentry would rush out to finish off the last wild tigers. Tata appeared nonplussed for once, but the book was already out in print.

I joined the Board High School in Puttur in the sixth grade directly, after passing a test administered by the school. Because we lived four kilometres away from the school, I could not play with my buddies after school hours. Weekends were spent alone, birdwatching in the Balavana woods or on the adjacent Padumale hillock.

Mine was a somewhat lonely boyhood. I longed for the holidays when I could go to Mangalore to spend time with my friend, Raghu, his sister Shyamala, and the rest of the Sathyashankar family. The fondest memories of my boyhood are rooted in Mangalore rather than in Puttur.

Sathyashankar (1920-95) and his wife Vasantha (1921-82) became my foster parents in Mangalore. I was very fond of Vasanthamma, who was like my surrogate mother. Their two children, Shyamala, a year older than me, and Raghu, who was my age, became my adopted siblings. Vasantha Sathyashankar, daughter of Mundkur Ekamabara Rao, and Amma were, of course, close friends from their Besant School days. Tata had taught both of them dance and drama. I thus had the privilege of truly belonging to two families.

Ullas's 'surrogate family' in Mangalore: The Satyashankars
Seated: Kanneppadi Satyashankar Rao, Vasanathamma (Vasantha
Satyashankar) Standing: Their son Raghu and daughter Shyamala

The Sathyashankars, being of Amma's age, having been trained as doctors in Madras, were far more cosmopolitan in their lifestyle. Theirs also was a love marriage like that of my parents. They were both leftist-rationalists, who also admired the philosopher Jiddu Krishnamurti.

My school friends in Puttur tended to be rather rustic in comparison to the new friends I made in Mangalore. My other bonds with the Mangalore boys was due to the hobby of pigeon racing. The pigeon racing we practised did not involve measuring the speed or the time it took for the racing bird to fly home after being released far away. Our mode of racing was to train the birds to fly very high, in sweeping circles around the loft, for hours on end. The better racing birds flew longer hours. Some of the champion birds could fly from dawn to dusk. Tata was happy to support my hobby and spent generously to build a pigeon loft in Balavana for my two dozen birds.

I also picked up my love for the game of cricket from Raghu, who was an excellent player. I was not as good, but did play cricket for my school in my final year.

I finished my matriculation (eleventh grade then) in 1964, passing with a first class. I had to leave Puttur to continue my college education. However, instead of going to MGM College in Udupi as my siblings had, I chose Mangalore. The Sathyashankars had warmly invited me to stay with them while I pursued the one-year Pre-University Course (PUC) in the academically acclaimed St. Aloysius College. Fifty-five years later, it was a very moving moment for me when the college recognised me among its distinguished alumni.

Because of my interest in animals, Tata suggested I should opt for biology rather than mathematics as an option in my PUC. I countered that if I opted for biology, the only decent career option would be to become a doctor and take care of sick human beings for the rest of my life. Not only were there no career options in wildlife, zoology taught at college level was dreary beyond belief. I chose mathematics instead, hoping to become an engineer with a decent job, pursuing natural history as a hobby.

After doing well in the PU examination, I gained admission to the National Institute of Technology, Karnataka (NITK) at Surathkal near Mangalore (then known as Karnataka Regional Engineering College).

Kshama and Ullas during their college days

The six years I spent with the Sathyashankars in Mangalore were transformational in many ways. Although they were both Brahmins (he a Havyaka and she a Chitrapur Saraswat), they were non-vegetarians and served alcohol at home. At age eighteen, I rapidly switched to their lifestyle, enjoying it thoroughly.

Tata had become a rationalist by choice in his early twenties. However, he remained a vegetarian and abhorred alcohol. Tata remained a vegetarian to avoid needless cruelty to animals, he said. He was also sure that alcohol inevitably led to one's ruination. This was based on his experience preaching temperance to rural folks at Mahatma Gandhi's urging. Tata had witnessed many rural poor families driven to misery because of alcoholism among the menfolk.

The Sathyashankars kept my conversion to their cosmopolitan lifestyle a secret from Tata to protect me from his anger.

Once I joined the coveted engineering college, I hated every minute spent in the classroom. I was not very good at my studies, although NITK was an excellent institution. A vast majority of the students were highly motivated. However, I chose to make my friends among the minority, who focused on having as much fun as possible without worrying about academic grades.

However, my love for the forests and wildlife remained deep-seated. Unlike my fellow hedonists, I did escape often to wild places like Kudremukh and Nagarahole to watch the vanishing wild animals. I disagreed with some of my friends who illegally hunted and wished they would get caught.

Although I was a mediocre engineer, I was pleasantly surprised when NITK recognised me as a distinguished alumnus on the institution's golden jubilee in 2010 for my contributions to wildlife conservation.

When I was in my final year at college, Tata heard from one of his friends that I drank alcohol. He urgently summoned me to Puttur. He said he had lost all hope for me, and broke down. I could not bear to see his sorrow. He made me promise that I would not touch alcohol while I was dependent on him. What I did with my life later was up to me, he said.

He had offered me an escape hatch. I promised Tata to follow his diktat, aware that my enforced temperance would last only till I got my first paycheck. In the years that followed, whenever he stayed at my home, I did not serve drinks. He was satisfied that I was not facing immediate ruination from alcohol as he had feared.

### Tata and my own family

I first met Prathibha Shetty in 1972 when we were both twenty-four. She worked as a speech pathologist at NIMHANS, Bangalore and was a friend of Malakka and her husband, Ravi Kapur.

She was a pretty, cheerful girl. She was a brilliant student who topped the university exams and later became an accomplished professional: a beauty with brains. Curiously, we had both been educated in Mangalore, living within two kilometres of each other's homes. Her cousin Mohandas Shetty was a good friend, a pigeon lover like me. I had even visited their sprawling 300-year-old Kodialguthu house. But we had never met.

Soon we became good friends and then fell in love. By 1973 we had decided to get married. Tata and Amma both knew Prathibha's mother Kausalia from their Besant School days. My parents were both fine with the idea of this alliance. So was Prathibha's father, Kaup Sarvotham Shetty, a well-known lawyer in Mangalore. He was a socialist labour lawyer in Madras in the 1950s. Shetty was one of the young members of the Radical Humanist Party that the revolutionary Manvendra Nath Roy founded after being ejected from the communist movement by Joseph Stalin. Other young 'Royists' with Shetty were V.M. Tarkunde, who later became a Supreme Court judge, and S.R. Bommai, who later became chief minister of Karnataka.

However, Prathibha's mother was unhappy about our alliance for the same reason that Amma's maternal uncle was unhappy when she married Tata thirty-eight years earlier. Kausalia Shetty was worried that she would lose face in her community, given the high status the Kodialguthu clan enjoyed.

While I was frustrated and upset with her resistance, Prathibha, the patient counsellor, cajoled her mother for a full year and wore her down until she agreed. Unlike me, Tata was sympathetic to the agony Prathibha's mother was going through. Amma, by then, was fully preoccupied with her own illnesses to care about all this.

Finally, when Kausalia Shetty agreed to our marriage, I felt happy and was ready for a quick civil ceremony or even a traditional Bunt wedding that entirely avoided Brahmin priests and Sanskrit mantras. However, my father-in-law sprang a surprise, perhaps to please the wider Karanth clan. He quietly organised a full-blown Brahmin style wedding. It was to be solemnised by a priest, with long hours of chanting of slokas before a sacred fire that belched much smoke. Desperate to get it over with, we all agreed.

Ullas and Prathibha get married in Mangalore following Brahminical rituals (left to right: the priest, Kaup Sarvotham Shetty [Prathibha's father], Ullas, Prathibha, Jyothi Alva [Prathibha's elder sister] and Kausalia Shetty [Prathibha's mother])

However, Tata had to go through the formal ritual of personally inviting members of the Karanth clan to my wedding, the memory of which amuses me hugely to this day.

Tata took me along through the lanes, gardens and rice paddies around Kota to distribute the wedding invitation to friends and relatives. We would walk into a home and Tata would hand over the invitation card. He would then loudly announce, 'Ullas is getting married in Mangalore. But you should not come.' With his elder brother K.L. Karanth, he used a more polite variant, saying, 'You should not bother about attending.' He would then go on and tell the invitees that 'they should not lose sleep over' the wedding ceremony because he was arranging a wedding feast in Kota a couple of days later. 'Do attend the feast without fail!' he admonished.

We then walked off to the home of the next 'invitee', leaving the last one entirely befuddled. To Tata's many friends and admirers far away, he sent printed 'invitation cards', with a handwritten note, similarly disinviting them.

Tata did not like the crowds, pomp and pageantry associated with traditional weddings. He just wanted my wedding over and out of the way.

After our wedding, however, things changed. Prathibha's entire clan, including her eighty-six-year-old grandmother, Rathna Rai, took me into their family warmly. It was amazing how quickly my mother-in-law's reservations melted away. I could even chat with a glass of rum in hand with my father-in-law, something I could never do with my own father!

Prathibha and I moved to Mysore in 1977. She was pursuing her PhD, while I decided to switch careers, buying a farm close to Nagarahole. I planned to spend time watching wildlife in the jungle for half the year when there was no work on the rainfed farm.

Tata used to visit Mysore on work a couple of times a year. Typically, he would spend an extra day relaxing with us. Prathibha took good care of his finicky dietary needs: small quantities of freshly cooked food, of different types, at each meal. Tata ate very little but was very finicky about what he ate.

Tata grew quite fond of Prathibha, perhaps because of her calm, balanced personality, in contrast to my testy Karanth temperament. He opened up and talked to her about things that he simply could not discuss with me. She did not question him or judge his actions like I sometimes did.

Prathibha recounts a couple of instances of how Tata, beneath his tough exterior, was a sensitive, subtly observant man. When she came as a bride to his home in Saligrama, she was fascinated by the *National Geographic* magazines in his library and spent hours reading them. Soon after, he quietly started mailing them to Prathibha.

Always a sharp dresser, Prathibha wore only sarees to work and when we stayed with our parents. And when Tata stayed at our home, Prathibha was always in a saree. At other times she liked to wear western clothes. She was pleasantly surprised by a gift Tata brought for her from Russia: a beautifully tailored lady's shirt that fitted her perfectly.

Tata's car trips, always with a driver at the wheel, typically lasted five or six days. Tata would visit different regions of Karnataka to give talks, preside over functions, participate in literary events and always drop in on his friends. If he was in southern Karnataka, he would invariably visit us at Mysore. Tata was incredibly punctual, following a schedule that he sent me well in advance. As Tata grew older, I kept telling him to avoid these longer trips.

One day in late 1987, when Tata did not reach our home from Tumakuru at 7 p.m. as he had promised, we were worried that the car may have broken down, or worse, met with an accident. In those pre-cellphone days, we could not check on him.

Finally, much to our relief, Tata turned up an hour late. Looking apologetic, he explained, 'Just as I finished my talk, a man approached me with the manuscript of a story he had written, seeking my comments. I could not refuse because he was so old (*thumba mudukaru*).' I asked Tata to guess how old the aspiring writer was. 'The poor man was at least seventy,' came the reply. Prathibha and I both burst out laughing, looking at the expression on his face when I asked him his own age. Tata was so full of life force that he never realised that he was eighty-five.

We moved back to Bangalore again in 1996. We had saved up a fair bit of money and bought a spacious duplex apartment. Prathibha and I were proud of our new home. Although Prathibha's parents had come and enjoyed staying with us, Tata had not. When Tata wrote about his upcoming trip in mid-1997, Prathibha insisted he stay with us. He liked our new apartment, particularly the roof garden that Prathibha had created, with a real grass lawn shaded by the canopy of a giant peepal tree taller than our building. He seemed taken aback when he found out how much it had cost. He was a frugal man, who always remembered the hard times he had endured in his youth.

Tata passed away a few months later.

6

# TATA'S CHARMED CIRCLE

K. Ullas Karanth

## Tata and his peers

Tata was a loner, a disciplined workaholic. Although he did not actively seek out friends, his magnetic personality, incredible talent and spontaneous wit attracted many of his peers and contemporaries to become his lifelong friends. What amazed me was how some of these friends were so different from Tata. Although Tata was a hypercritical overachiever, he was remarkably flexible in the kind of friends he made. While listing all of them here is impossible, I have tried to mention some whose deep bonds with Tata I witnessed first-hand.

One among them was India's foremost painters, Kattingeri Krishna Hebbar (K.K. Hebbar [1911-96]) from Udupi, who had migrated to Bombay in the 1930s and made his reputation as a modern artist. Tata visited Bombay to explore the art world and soon Hebbar and he became close, lifelong friends.

Hebbar often contributed line drawings or paintings for Tata's books. Tata stayed with Hebbar during his Bombay visits, spending long hours in his studio. When I visited Bombay, I too stayed with the Hebbars. After the 1980s, when Hebbar visited Mysore, he would stay at our home. He had a rather delicate stomach, and Prathibha could cook mildly spiced meals precisely the way he liked.

Tata and the eminent artist, K.K. Hebbar, their friendship
and mutual admiration going back five decades

Tata sometimes tried his hand at creating drawings or paintings for his own books. Of course, the results were simply not in the same league as Hebbar's work. After seeing one of Tata's illustrations, Hebbar once plaintively complained to me: 'Ullas, why does your Tata insist on doing these atrocious illustrations? He knows that I will drop everything on hand to illustrate his works. You must somehow convince him to stop this practice.'

In his final few years in Saligrama, Tata had a telephone installed under intense pressure from all of us. However, to avoid being bothered by unsolicited calls, he sought refuge in a little-known legal provision to enable only outward calls on his phone. Once a week, at a fixed time, Tata would call Malakka, Kshama and me. The only other call he made was to K.K. Hebbar.

Another long-term friend of Tata was Gundugutti Manjanthaiah

(1904-86), a coffee planter from Kodagu. G.M. Manjanathaiah admired Tata's writings and shared his anti-socialist political stance. Manjanathaiah's grandfather was one of the first local planters who adopted the British style, large-scale commercial cultivation of coffee in South India. The coffee plant had been a back garden crop until the mid-nineteenth century.

Tata's close friend and supporter—coffee planter G. M. Manjanathaiah of Kodagu, with his wife Meenakshiamma. Staying in their bungalow, Tata wrote some of his great novels.

In the 1950s, Manjanathaiah was perhaps the largest individual coffee planter in Kodagu, holding over two thousand acres of prime Arabica coffee. He had built a beautiful western-style mansion near Suntikoppa, which was surrounded by lush green landscaped lawns and rose gardens.

I looked forward to our visits to the Gundugutti mansion. My first ritual upon reaching was to rush upstairs to the huge library with wooden flooring, to admire the mounted trophy of a leopard that Manjanthaiah had hunted years before. I also ogled the three fancy American cars our hosts owned: a Pontiac, a Packard and a Studebaker.

The only incongruous elements in that British-style mansion were the kitchen and the large dining room at the back. The entire household had its meals there, sitting on the floor cross-legged to partake delicious Havyaka Brahmin meals served on plantain leaves.

Manjanathiah and his outspoken but warm-hearted wife, Meenakshiamma (1909-94), were among Tata's closest friends. Some of Tata's early novels like *Bettada Jeeva* (Man from the Mountain)[47] were written when he took time off to stay with them. At the end of each day, Tata read out his literary output to the couple.

Manjanathaiah's sons, Gopalakrishna and Mohan, also loved and respected Tata. The entire family was deeply involved in politics. Manjanthaiah was elected as a Congress legislator in the 1950s but got disenchanted with the Congress party. Later he switched his support to the right-wing opposition parties. Manjanathaiah was a major leader of the Swatantra Party in Karnataka. Gopalakrishna (1927-2014) was aligned with the Jan Sangh and hobnobbed with the likes of Atal Behari Vajpayee, whereas Mohan (1933-1988) was a friend of the Swatantra Party leader, Piloo Mody.

Manjanathaiah was an extraordinarily generous man, giving away large sums of money to public charities and in private donations to all sorts of causes and people in distress. Many of Tata's major ventures, such as his first trip to Europe in 1952, narrated in his travelogue *Apoorva Paschima* (The Wonderful Occident)[48], the production of his science encyclopedia, *Vijnana Prapancha*[49], as well as the purchase of machines for the printing press, were all financed by the interest-free loans from Manjanathaiah. Tata later diligently repaid these loans.

Another long-term friendship Tata developed was with the Pais

---

47   See B-33 in Annotated Bibliography for more details
48   See B-35 in Annotated Bibliography for more details
49   See B-28 in Annotated Bibliography for more details

of Manipal. They built up the massive global conglomerate of world-class educational institutions and businesses we see today, starting from scratch on the barren hillocks of Manipal in South Kanara.

The founders of the Manipal dynasty were brothers Upendra Pai (1895-1956) and Madhava Pai (1898-1979). They were visionaries who started the Syndicate Bank as well as several hospitals and educational institutions. When the Pai brothers innovated the model of a capitation fee-based medical college in the early 1950s, the University of Mysore refused to grant them the necessary academic affiliation. However, because of his literary stature and fight for the unification of Karnataka, Tata had many friends in northern Karnataka. One such friend was C.C. Hulkoti, then vice-chancellor of the Karnatak University in Dharwad. After Tata and the Pai brothers jointly pleaded the cause of the medical college, the affiliation was granted. The rest is history.

Among the Pais of the next generation, T.A. Pai (1922-81), who was India's industries minister under Indira Gandhi, T. Ramesh Pai (1924-2005), who headed the Manipal conglomerate and their youngest brother, the free-spirited T. Ganesh Pai (all sons of Upendra Pai) and M. Ramdas Pai (1935-), son of Madhava Pai, were all Tata's friends and admirers.

When I was a little boy, our family visited Manipal occasionally. The first air-conditioned room I spent time in was Madhava Pai's bedroom, where he sat and chatted with Tata and Amma. When T.A. Pai's first marriage broke up, Tata and Amma had joined the family's effort to heal the breach.

The Pai family reciprocated Tata's friendship in ample measure. They supported Tata in many of his creative endeavours in Udupi and Manipal. They also provided incredible long-term medical support to Amma during her many years of illnesses, virtually free of cost. Tata was particularly fond of Ramesh Pai, who, despite his busy schedule as the head of the conglomerate, would drop in to see Amma whenever she was a patient at the hospital.

The senior generation of Pais would often stop over in Puttur to visit Tata en route to Bangalore. Ganesh Pai was a frequent visitor. He was a very bright, jovial and unconventional man. A vegan, he invented gadgets of all kinds and was also an amateur Yakshagana dancer. Unfortunately, he died relatively early while undergoing a cardiac procedure.

Unfortunately, Tata's personally warm relationship with T.A. Pai ended when the latter contested as a Congress candidate from Udupi in the 1977 parliamentary election. Tata, because of his opposition to the Emergency earlier imposed by Indira Gandhi, felt compelled to campaign against his friend of many years.

Another long-term friendship Tata had was with the remarkable industry pioneer in Mangalore, Vamana Kudva (1899-1967), who is today hardly remembered outside Mangalore. Kudva's Canara Public Conveyance Company (CPC) once owned the largest fleet of buses and trucks in southern India. He was the first Indian industrialist to master the continuous casting steel technology, a process essential for making leaf springs for automobiles. Every car manufactured in India had Kudva's Canara Springs as original equipment.

A versatile technocrat, Kudva also published the first mass circulation daily newspaper in Kanara, *Navabharatha*, employing imported American machinery. He also wrote *Motaru Yanthra Vijnana*, possibly the first Kannada book on automobile engineering.

At its peak, Kudva's industrial enterprises rivalled those of the contemporaneous TVS group of Madras. However, unlike the TVS group, Kudva's industrial conglomerate declined after he passed away.

Tata, who had given up on Gandhi and his anti-industry notions in the 1930s, admired Vamana Kudva because of his own deep interest in technology and industrial development. As it happened, Kudva's youngest son, Balakrishna, and I became very close friends in engineering college (we still are). I used to greet Vamana Kudva with reverence whenever I visited his home to see my friend.

Another successful businessman friend of Tata was Moodbidre

Authors at work on *Growing Up Karanth*: Ullas Karanth, Malavika Kapur, Kshama Rau

Tata, the idealist freedom fighter and social reformer (seated third from left), with like-minded friends, including Tadagaje Nagesha Rao (seated, extreme left).

Tata's family in Kota: Standing L to R: Lakshminarayana, Ramakrishna (elder brothers), Shesha Karanth (father), Shankarnarayana, Narasimha (younger brothers) and Tata. Seated L to R: Younger brother Shivayya, younger sister Yamuna, mother Mahalakshmi, younger sister Shridevi and the youngest brother Parameshwara.

Amma and her family: Sitting on the ground L to R: Amma, elder sister Savithri, younger sister Rathna. Seated on the chairs: Younger sister Ahalya, uncle Mundappa Poonja and his wife 'Neliyappe', grandmother Akkamma, stepmother Pushpavathi and father Kamu Tyampanna Alva. At the back: Amma's youngest sister, Sarojini, carried by a house help.

As a young student in Besant Girls High School, Mangalore,
Amma excelled in her studies, sports, drama and dance.

Our family in Balavana in the early 1950s: Harshanna,
Amma, Kshama, Malavika, Tata, Ullas

The literary giants, Tata's friends: V.K. Gokak, Masti Venkatesha Iyengar

Our cousin Sooryanarayana Karanth—'Sooryanna'—who was like a
sibling to  all three of us, and like a son to our parents,
with his wife Sumathi

Malavika finds her life's partner in Ravi Kapur

Malavika's family: Ravi, Malavika (with daughter Svapna in her arms)
with Ullas, Kshama and Amma, in Balavana

Malavika's son Sharad's wedding. Standing: Ullas, Ravi, Stella (Sharad's wife), Sharad, Samir. Seated: Krithi, Malavika and Svapna, holding her son Nishant.

Karanth family in the mid-1960s: Malavika, Tata, Ullas, Amma and Kshama.

We always had pet dogs in Balavana ranging from pure-bred German Shepherds to cross-breeds of various kinds. Playing with Amma and Tata are two of these pets, Malavika's Spaniel-Dachshund Jim on the left and the German Shepherd Moti belonging to Ullas and Kshama on the right.

Prathibha and Ullas at Bandipur, 1974

Our long-term family friendship with the Pais of Manipal; the picture was taken in Balavana in the 1950s. Back row: Amma, Tonse Madhava Pai, Tata and a friend. Front row: girl from the friend's family, Kshama, boy from the friend's family, Raghu Ram (Sathyashankar's son), Ullas, Shyamala (Sathyashankar's daughter).

Eminent writer and public intellectual U. R. Ananthamurthy was inspired by Tata, and maintained an affectionate relationship with him over the years.

Tata playing the role of the director while shooting *Maleya Makkalu* based on his acclaimed novel *Kudiyara Koosu*.

Serving Tata with trust and affection. L to R: Driver Ananda Poojari, cook Rama Mogera, Malavika, relative Krishna Karanth and his wife Vedavathi. In the background is the museum established in Tata's honour in Kota, with assistance from the Government of Karnataka.

Ullas with Krithi and Tata in Nagarahole Wildlife Reserve

Ullas at work: pioneering advanced research on wild tigers in India

Ullas with his mentor at the Wildlife Conservation Society (WCS), George Schaller.
Holding the plaque of the 'George Schaller Award' instituted by WCS.

Ramakrishna Hegde, chief minister of Karnataka, was a great admirer of Tata.
During 1989, Hegde and prime minister Rajiv Gandhi felicitated Tata at the
Vishwa Kannada Sammelana (World Kannada Conference) in Mysore.

A lifelong struggle for the cause of Kannada. Tata addressing the Vishwa Kannada Sammelana (World Kannada Conference) at Mysore in 1989. Dignitaries on the stage listening with rapt attention include: campaigner for Kannada B.G. Banakar, Kannada movie icon Rajkumar, the Mayor of Mysore city, former chief ministers R. Gundu Rao and S. Nijalingappa, poet K.V. Puttappa (Kuvempu), Tata, former chief minister and vice-president of India B.D. Jatti, chief minister Ramakrishna Hegde and cabinet minister B. Rachaiah.

Travelling with Tata, observing and understanding art and architecture was an experience that enriched all three of us greatly.

Many accolades came Tata's way in recognition of his accomplishments.
Tata receiving the high civilian honour Padma Bhushan from the president of India,
Dr Zakir Hussain, in 1968. He renounced the award later, protesting the national
Emergency declared by Indira Gandhi in 1975.

Tata had a wide range of interests, as captured brilliantly in this line drawing
by K.K. Hebbar. He exposed us to all these domains, enabling us to focus
and choose what we ultimately did in our lives.

Tata experimented with Yakshagana, innovating creatively. He demonstrated his dance form on his 90th birthday celebrated in the Kota High School, with eminent Yakshagana exponent Hiriyadka Gopala Rao playing the maddale (drum).

Innovation within a tradition: Tata refined the Yakshagana tradition to create his 'Yaksharanga' format, which could reach out globally, going beyond Karnataka.

Innovation and experimentation within the Odissi dance tradition:
Kshama with her Guru Kelucharan Mahapatra

Kshama demonstrating Odissi dance tradition at the Sun Temple in Konark, Odisha.

'Vision Karanth' of Kshama: Restoration work in progress for the Shivarama Karanth lifestyle museum in Balavana, Puttur

The unique privilege of 'growing up Karanth': Kshama, Ullas and Malavika

Sanjiva Rao (1909-82). After migrating to Bombay at a young age, Rao had thrived in the automobile spare parts business. He was a leader among the Kannadigas of Bombay and a driving force behind many of their cultural and social institutions. Rao was also a philanthropist who lived unostentatiously. When Harshanna was hospitalised in Bombay before his death, Sanjiva Rao and his family stood rock-like in support of Tata and Amma.

A friendship of Tata's that I found difficult to fathom was with a wealthy landlord, Hasanagi Ganapathy Bhat (1903-70) from Manchikeri in North Kanara. Bhat, who owned vast arecanut plantations, was a connoisseur of arts, literature and fine food. He and his many relatives lived in one of the traditional long houses called Salu Mane in the hilly regions of North Kanara. In that architectural arrangement, dozens of family homes are conjoined sideways and under a single roof, while sharing a continuous chavadi (veranda) that extends over 80 metres in length. Tata had explained to me that this architecture was devised to fight off Maratha brigands during their periodic looting forays into Kanara.

In any case, behind the ornately carved wooden pillars of the chavadi, the interiors of these homes were dark dungeons filled with wood smoke generated by the enormous meals cooked by the army of women slaving inside. The men gathered on the chavadi at the end of the day to listen to Tata read out excerpts from his books or demonstrate his dance-dramas. Men would have debates on philosophy, art and politics, which Tata dominated through sheer lung power. Ganapathy Bhat, however, used to bluntly tell Tata, 'I do not agree that there is no god, even if a brilliant man like you says so.' They never argued that point further.

To me, the special attraction of visits to Hasanagi were the twenty-seven leopard skins (including two melanistic black ones) and the two tigers-skins spread over the chairs in the upper storey. All had been hunted by Bhat and his relatives over the years. The last of these tiger hunts occurred in 1965, and Bhat had presented the skin to Tata. It is still in my possession. The DNA extracted from that skin has recently contributed to the study of tiger evolution in the Indian subcontinent.

Another areca planter friend of Tata's, closer home in Puttur, was Kuppuluchar Mari Bhat. A few years older than Tata, he was a wealthy planter, who, however, dressed quite shabbily in a crumpled shirt and a white mundu, from the underneath of which the tail of his colourful loin cloth would hang out. But his shabby persona hid a curious mind.

Mari Bhat visited Balavana to spend hours talking to Tata about everything in the world. When Tata quietly crept away to his work desk, Mari Bhat would switch his attention to Amma. Despite his rusticity, Mari Bhat was well-read on international affairs. He had a particular fascination for the Second World War. I recall listening to him with rapt attention as Mari Bhat expounded at length and with great authority about the battlefield tactics of German field marshals Gerd Von Rundstedt and Erwin Rommel. He would occasionally take a break, dash out of the house, spit out a great plume of blood-red betel juice and return to his discourse on military history.

Another cultured man close to the Karanth family was Agrala Purandara Rai, a progressive farmer from Punacha village, who was also a writer, poet and journalist. Rai was a very tall, gaunt man, a striking personality with a deep booming voice. Tata enjoyed discussing literature and folk arts with him and listening to Rai's recital of his own poems. Rai's son, Viveka Rai, a couple of years senior to me at school, became a well-known Kannada scholar, retiring as the vice chancellor of Kannada University at Hampi.

Belle Ramachandra Rao, a lawyer who also dabbled in English poetry, dropped in occasionally for literary discussions. Although Rao had never visited England, his poems were mostly about the beauty of daffodils and other such charms of the English countryside.

Then there was the regular gang of Tata's old friends. The word 'gang' is perhaps too strong to describe these gentle souls in their fifties and sixties. Every evening Tata would walk from Balavana to

Puttur town. He held court around a desk at the corner of a large shop owned by his friend, Shridhar Bhat. They would meet, share cups of tea, discuss current affairs and disperse. Tata would walk home with the previous day's *The Times of India* from Bombay, while I waited eagerly to read its last page that featured the Tarzan comic strip by Edgar Rice Burroughs.

One of the members of this gang was a Havyaka landlord and literary aficionado, Ademane Palathadka ('A.P.') Subbayya. He was a frail hypochondriac who, apparently, in his youth, was a formidable hockey player who had represented Coorg (Kodagu). He had a penchant for translating Western classics into Kannada. Masterpieces like *Les Miserables*, *The Vicar of Wakefield* and *David Copperfield* were some of them. The friendship between Karanth and the AP family has now extended into the third generation.

Another regular member of the gang was a gentle Saraswat high school teacher, Tadagaje Nagesh Rao. When Tata was getting sucked into the freedom struggle in Mangalore in 1922, Rao, a high school student, came under his sway. Sometimes he would persuade Rao not to go back home, but to accompany him to Balavana. As they entered the house, Tata would call out to Amma, 'Leela, come out, saadhugalu (the saintly one) is joining us for dinner tonight.' Nagesh Rao was a pious man and he and Amma chatted for hours about spiritual matters. For Kshama and me, the Ganesha Chowthi Pooje in the Tadagaje home performed with two Ganesha idols, followed by a sumptuous feast, was the high point of the year.

The third permanent member of the gang was the tall, lanky retired headmaster, Kallianpur Bhavanishankar Rao (also see chapter 8). Rao's son, Gopinath Kallianpur, was an eminent statistician who settled in the US, while also serving a stint as the director of the Indian Statistical Institute. When Tata visited the US years later, Gopi Kallianpur took time off to drive him around the country and show him the Grand Canyon and other spectacles.

When I dropped in to see Gopiyanna at Chapel Hill,

North Carolina in 2004, he looked stunned: the fifty-six-year-old man facing him looked nothing like the Ullas he remembered from three decades earlier!

## *Those inspired by Tata*

Tata inspired hundreds of talented men and women in the generations that followed him. Much has been written about him by many of them. My focus here is on a few such individuals whom I personally got to know well in later years.

Prabhashankar Rao Padukone (1923-2014, Ramananda Rao's son, Tata's old mentor [see chapter 1, section entitled 'Mentors of the Renaissance Man']) got to know Tata well. He was a boy during the days Tata stayed in their home. He was a widely read man, deeply interested in music, both Indian and western classical. Padukone was also a well-known Kannada humorist. His collection of essays, *Telibanda Yelegalu* (Leaves That Floated By),[50] contains some very touching accounts of how Tata mentored him. I was fortunate to hang out with him in New York City for a few days in 1989 when Padukone was chaperoning Tata around. His wife, Vrinda Padukone (née Mundkur), was a childhood friend of Amma's (chapter 2).

Of the same vintage was H.Y. Sharada Prasad (1924-2008), a firebrand student leader in Mysore during the 1942 Quit India movement. He was a Nehruvian idealist who later became an official in the inner circles of the Nehru–Gandhi dynasty. Sharada Prasad admired Tata greatly. Tata was very fond of him and his wife Kamalamma, and stayed in their official residence near Lodi Gardens when he was in Delhi. Later, when I visited Delhi for work, their home became my refuge too. Although Tata was vehemently opposed to Indira Gandhi, his friendship with Sharada Prasad, who was her key advisor, never frayed.

---

50   See B-12 in Annotated Bibliography for more details

H.Y. Sharada Prasad (right) looks on as eminent scholar,
Kapila Vatsyayan (left), honours Tata. Although Prasad was
a trusted senior advisor to Indira Gandhi whom Tata opposed,
that never came in the way of friendship between them.

In one instance, when Tata took Sharada Prasad's two boys, Ravi and Sanjiva, for a walk in the Lodi Gardens, a perfect stranger stopped them and asked Tata if the boys were his grandchildren. Without batting an eye, Tata had replied, 'No, but they are indeed grand children!'

Another eminent cultural figure who was similarly inspired by Tata was the Ramon Magsaysay Award winner, K.V. Subbanna (1932-2005). His contributions to Kannada literature, theatre and the performing arts, all the while based in the little village of Heggodu deep in the Western Ghats, are well-known. Subbanna was a rationalist like Tata, but unlike Tata, he was also a socialist. However, their shared interests and bonds of affection ensured that these ideological differences mattered little. I remember Subbanna's visits to Puttur during my school days. I have visited Heggodu with Tata in my boyhood and have continued that tradition over the years to watch with admiration how Subbanna's son (and my friend), K.V. Akshara, is expanding his father's cultural quests in multiple dimensions.

Tata, flanked by K.V. Subbanna (R) and Padaru Mahabaleshwara Bhat (L)
who assisted Tata in his folklore research.

Tata was also an inspiration to three other next-generation stars of Kannada literature, theatre and culture: U.R. Ananthamurthy, Girish Karnad and B.V. Karanth. It was only after I got to know them well later that I realised how profound Tata's influence had been on them during their formative years and how much they stood in genuine awe of Tata's pioneering intellectual and personal explorations despite their ideological differences with him.

Among the trio, Tata was personally very fond of Ananthamurthy (1932-2014). When Tata was in Mysore, he would always drop in for a cup of coffee with Murthy. Basking in Tata's reflected glory, Prathibha and I too have benefited much from Ananthamurthy's incredible affection and charming erudition.

Although B.V. Karanth made a brilliant film based on Tata's famous novel *Chomana Dudi*,[51] Tata had not liked the film. B.V. Karanth, a warm, good-hearted man and a true genius of Kannada

---

51    See B-36 in Annotated Bibliography for more details

theatre, in contrast to Tata, was somewhat undisciplined and often unpunctual. I suspect Tata's dislike of that outstanding movie had more to do with B.V. Karanth's disorganised persona. B.V. Karanth had once confessed to me that he was 'scared of' Tata.

Because Tata was a jack of all trades who dabbled in anything that took his fancy, some of his prolific intellectual output tended to be mediocre. Since Tata did not like B.V. Karanth's film, he set out to make a better movie based on another acclaimed novel of his, *Kudiyara Koosu.*[52] Prathibha and I spent a couple of days on the sets when this movie, titled *Maleya Makkalu,* was filmed in a very scenic forested landscape in the Western Ghats. Although the scenery was grand and the movie starred the popular Kannada actress Kalpana, the movie was a rather amateurish effort compared to *Chomana Dudi.* Tata's film failed the test of critical appreciation, and at the box office.

Another writer of the Ananthamurthy–Karnad–Karanth generation was poet K.V. Puttappa's (Kuvempu) son Poornachandra Tejaswi (1938-2007). He was a leading Kannada writer who genuinely shared Tata's wider interests in nature and photography. Because of my own interest in the same topics, I got to know Tejaswi fairly well in the 1980s. Tata met him a few years later, and from the word go, they got along really well. Tejasvi later told me it was his eternal regret that he did not reach out and get to know Tata much earlier. Tata's wide range of interests, passion and frankness had greatly impressed Tejaswi.

## Admirers who stood by Tata

While Tata's energy and enterprise were at the core of his accomplishments in many fields, much credit should also go to individuals who supported and served him in many ways. They adored him for his achievements or simply loved him as a person. Some of them are public figures, while others are not. The list below is a filtered sample of individuals I knew well.

---

52   See B-37 in Annotated Bibliography for more details

One such friend was K.S. Haridas Bhat (1924-2003), a teacher of economics and the principal of MGM College in Udupi. He was Tata's right-hand man for many years, deeply involved in many of his endeavours. Bhat possessed a bright intellect and a marvellous sense of humour. He was an extraordinarily capable manager of men and materials. He was a major force in establishing the Shivarama Karanth library and the famous Yakshagana Kendra Training Centre in MGM college. He travelled the world managing the Yaksharanga dance troupes, winning many accolades for Tata.

Gundmi Ramakrishna Aithal (1933-93), a prominent hotelier in Bangalore, was another pillar of support for Tata after the 1960s, right until his own death. Aithal had migrated from Kota to escape poverty when he was nine and worked in small restaurants in Davanagere and Sagara, and was briefly jailed during the freedom struggle. He established himself as a successful hotelier in Bangalore after 1950.

Admirers and friends who stood by Tata—Mallikarjunaiah
and Gundmi Ramakrisha Aithal

Aithal had a deep interest in literature. After he prospered in life, Aithal befriended and generously supported many literary figures in

Bangalore. However, Tata was special to Aithal not only because of his literary accomplishments but also because of their shared roots in Kota.

When Tata turned sixty, his fans had organised a series of celebratory events in towns and cities across Karnataka. Aithal, who was still growing his business, watched and waited. When Tata turned sixty-six, Aithal organised a series of grand celebratory events on his own steam and endeared himself to Tata. In the early 1970s, when Tata decided to leave Puttur and settle near Kota, Aithal advanced his plan for building a bungalow near Kota for his own eventual retirement. Aithal generously invited Tata to live in his bungalow, 'Suhasa', in Saligrama, for as long as Tata wanted to.

Whenever Tata visited Bangalore, a constant presence by his side was M. Mallikarjunaiah, a senior officer in the directorate of technical education. Ever so polite, gentle and kind, Mallikarjunaiah was a bachelor who took it upon himself to 'get things done' for Tata. Tata had to only say the word and Mallikarjunaiah would unctuously respond, '*Aagali Saar, xxx avarige heli madisabahudu*' (Sure sir, I will talk to Sri. xxx and get that done). The '*xxx*' could have been a prominent minister, a senior official or even a religious seer belonging to the Lingayat community.

Amma used to joke that Mallikarjunaiah played the role of Hanumantha to Tata's Rama. The only favour Mallikarjunaiah ever sought in return for all his services was to be allowed to take Tata to the famous restaurant, Mavalli Tiffin Room (MTR), near Lal Bagh. On those occasions, Mallikarjunaiah and his friends enjoyed Tata's company and banter under the benign supervision of the Mayyas of Kota who owned that bespoke eatery.

These admirers, and others like them, were the pillars who provided stability to Tata's illustrious career.

### In Tata's loyal service

There were some other exceptional individuals employed by Tata at various times whose contributions are known only to a few of us. They were as close to Tata as his own family members. While Kshama and

I were growing up, these handful of individuals were the bulwark support to our family. I can particularly mention four of them: press employee Narayana Manjeshwara, cook and helper Rama Mogera, literary scribe Girija Kulal and car driver Ananda Poojary.

Naranyana Manjeshwara (chapter 2) came into the Karanth household in April 1947 as a ten-year-old boy, accompanying his mother Ammanni Belchappada who had been hired as a domestic help. Their family lived in a thatched hut in Tata's nine-acre property, 'Harshavana', on which the government rest house in Puttur stands today. Because Narayana was so bright and hardworking, Amma asked him to stay at our home in Balavana.

Narayana assisted Amma in her daily household chores. He also worked part-time in the printing press. He was a talented young man and a voracious reader. My entire exposure to the epic Mahabharata in boyhood was from Narayana reading aloud the Kannada version of that classic by A.R. Krishna Shastri. No version of Mahabharata I have seen in films or on TV now can match that experience.

During the mid-1950s, half a dozen young men employed in Harsha Printery were swayed by the rising Communist Party of India. Following the revelations after De-Stalinisation in Russia, Tata had come to abhor communism. The printing press was not making much profit either, and the salaries he paid were low. When the employees abstained from work, demanding higher wages, Tata shuttered down the press. Sadly, Narayana, who had joined the strike, had to leave our home.

Decades later, Narayana, who had set up his own small printing presses, first in Vittala and then in Bangalore, reconnected with me. His booklet titled *Karantharondige Kelavu Varshagalu*, about the years he spent with our family, is a deeply moving personal account of his life when he lived with us.[53]

Rama Mogera of Kota (1937-) is unlikely to similarly record his yeomen service to our family. He first came to Balavana

---

53   See B-25 in Annotated Bibliography for more details

as a cook and caretaker in the mid-1950s. Rama was a fit, hard-working young man from the fisherfolk community. At Balavana, although there existed a social hierarchy, there was no caste-based distinction. Rama tried hard, I confess not very successfully, to inculcate some discipline into the utterly spoilt brats that Kshama and I were at that time.

When Harshanna was hospitalised in Bombay with a malignant tumour in 1960, requiring Amma and Tata's presence by his side, Rama returned to Balavana for a second spell to look after Kshama and me. When the telegram arrived informing us that Harshanna was no more, it was Rama who consoled us.

After returning from Bombay, Amma's mental health deteriorated rapidly. Soon she was clinically diagnosed as a manic-depressive and put on a sedative drug called Largactil. One afternoon, when Tata was away in Subramanya, Amma's mood turned suicidal. She went out telling Rama she was going to the town, saying she would return with Tata. When she did not return as promised, Rama went in search of her.

He found her in the mango orchard in Balavana, barely conscious, after having deliberately overdosed on the drug Largactil. Rama carried her home, and leaving her in the care of 'Hotel Ajji' (chapter 8), cycled to the town to meet Tata who was returning from his trip. The family doctor (and our relative), Sathyasundar Rao, managed to bring Amma back from the brink.

Later, Tata helped Rama get a job in a bank. When Tata relocated to Saligrama in 1972, Rama reconnected with our family and continued to assist Tata by running errands for him.

Tata's handwriting in Kannada was almost illegible. Therefore, he began to 'dictate' his books to 'scribes' who took dictation in longhand. Tata then corrected the drafts in red ink, and the scribe would prepare a final clean copy for publication. That was it: within a week or ten days the novel would be ready for print.

Several young ladies worked as Tata's scribes, sequentially, over the years. Usually, after working for a couple of years, they got married and moved on. One among them, Girija Kulal (chapter 2), however, stayed on for many years and became a part of our family. 'Girija Teacher', as we called her, had taught me mathematics at home before I joined high school.

Girija was a warm-hearted, kind lady. Amma and she were fond of each other. Later Girija found a regular job as a school teacher, got married and moved to Chennai where she connected with Kshama again. Her bond with our family continued until she died in her eighties. Girija was a writer of some merit and her account of Tata, Amma and their relationship is a truly moving narrative.[54]

Last to enter our lives as one of these remarkable subalterns to Tata was Ananda Poojary (1942-) from Parpunja village near Puttur, who was a Billava by caste. He joined as Tata's car driver in 1963 and soon became his man Friday. Ananda was a hardworking man with multiple talents: he was a skilled mechanic, a book binder, a horticulturist and much else. Everyone in Tata's circle of friends and admirers treated Ananda like a member of our family. Tata treated him almost like a son. He was an incredibly upright, honest and dependable prop to Tata for twenty-two years before Tata terminated his services under the unfortunate circumstances described in chapter 10.

Ananda has written a very frank personal account of his association and his final estrangement from Tata. Some of it was published in the magazine *Taranga*.[55] Ananda later told me the editor had tempered its frankness by several notches. Ananda's handwritten manuscript still bears witness to that fact. Ananda has continually and affectionately kept in touch with me and my siblings to this day, despite his estrangement from Tata.

I see Tata as a century-old giant peepal tree which grew drawing nourishment from roots such as the stellar examples of his mentors, contemporaries, admirers and subalterns whom I have presented above.

---

54   See B-24 in Annotated Bibliography for more details
55   See B-37 in Annotated Bibliography for more details

# 7

# ENGAGING WITH THE REAL WORLD

*K. Ullas Karanth*

## *Tata and my working life*

When I graduated from engineering college in 1971, T.A. Pai of Manipal suggested to Tata that I should join as a management trainee in a new company in Bombay that a friend of his had launched. When Tata asked me, I politely declined the offer because I desired to be based not too far from the jungles I loved. In hindsight, I often wonder where my career would have taken me had I accepted Pai's offer: the aforementioned friend was the entrepreneur Dhirubhai Ambani who was just beginning his meteoric rise, perhaps with some help from Pai. I am glad I did, because my life would not have been the wild and wonderful one I have enjoyed in the five decades since.

Like Tata in his youth, I too am a free-spirited individual, bent on pursuing my passions. After suffering two years of regimentation in Robert Bosch (then known as Motor Industries Company or MICO) in Bangalore, I got bored and quit. G.M. Mohan, Manjanathaiah's son (chapter 6), took me under his wing like a brother and employed me in his company that sold farm equipment. Two years later, I disappointed him by leaving the job to take up farming. Although Tata was pleased that I was 'independent', others thought I was crazy.

When I took up tobacco farming in Mysore district in 1976, Ajith Vombatkere, a tobacco company executive, became my close friend and mentor. Coincidentally, I learned that Ajith was, in fact, the grandson of the Saraswat ICS pioneer Vombatkere Pandrang Row (chapter 1).

It took me two more decades of persistent effort to switch my professional career entirely to wildlife biology: first graduating from the University of Florida, and then being hired to work in India for the New York-based Wildlife Conservation Society (WCS). Tata was truly happy at this outcome.

Tata had originally seeded this interest in natural history in my heart. In 1963, he had given me George Schaller's book on gorillas, saying, 'Read about this remarkable man and his dedication to wildlife.' Once again, it was in Tata's collection of *LIFE* magazines in 1965 that I read Schaller's article titled 'My Year With Tigers', which made me set my heart on becoming a tiger biologist. This chain of events came full circle when George Schaller recruited me off the University of Florida campus to join WCS in 1988 at the ripe old age of forty.

Tata visited me in Nagarahole a few times during the decades I conducted my tiger research. In 1994, I was even able to track and show him a wild tigress I had fitted with a radio collar. On another one of his trips, my daughter Krithi, then in her teens, Tata and I sat on a watchtower. Krithi showed off her wildlife-spotting prowess, being the first to detect a leopard stalking some monkeys at a great distance. She felt very proud that she had beaten me in 'game spotting' right before 'Tatajja', whom she adored.

Using family connections to advance one's career is the norm in India, whether it is in politics, industry or entertainment. At the outset of my career, I had noted how Tata had made a name for himself without seeking patronage from his family. I was determined not to use Tata's name to promote my own career. I think he appreciated this attitude.

I did, however, seek his help in some public conservation causes, and he readily obliged. In 1980, a small band of us wildlife conservationists in Mysore were protesting the construction of a luxury wildlife lodge that would have disrupted elephant movements in the Kabini river area of Nagarhole. The project was actively promoted by the then chief minister, R. Gundu Rao, who was an acolyte of Indira Gandhi's all-powerful son, Sanjay. When all else failed, I decided to use Tata as a weapon. I wrote up a carefully crafted appeal against the project addressed to Indira Gandhi and convinced Tata to sign it. I then got the writer R.K. Narayan also to sign it. Narayan was genuinely interested in wildlife and had borrowed my tiger books for reference when he wrote his novel *A Tiger for Malgudi*. Next, I persuaded writer U.R. Anathamurthy to endorse the appeal. Thereafter, I mailed their joint appeal to Tata's friend, H.Y. Sharada Prasad, following this up with a long-distance phone call. This strategy worked: Indira Gandhi ordered Gundu Rao to review the project. Eventually, the Kabini lodge was moved out from the Masthigudi corridor to its present location in Karapura village.

Another crisis arose in 1988 when I was a student in Florida. Local poachers and other vested interests around Nagarhole conspired to foist a false charge of abetment to murder on my friend, forest ranger Chinnappa, when a forest guard shot a local planter after an altercation. Chinnappa was a tough, strict ranger whom the local poachers hated. The efforts of the forest department to protect Chinnappa from unfair police persecution were failing because of strong local political pressures. I connected with Tata from the US, knowing well that the state chief minister, Ramakrishna Hegde, respected him greatly. Tata wrote a strong letter to Hegde, saying persecution of an upright official like Chinnappa was a blot on his government. Hegde intervened to order a special police enquiry which fully exonerated Chinnappa. Later, Chinnappa even received a medal for meritorious service from Hegde.

In the last decade of Tata's life, I was obsessively immersed in my own tiger research project. I was breaking new scientific ground as well as dealing with many problems, including political harassment and slander that came my way because of my attempts to practice both conservation advocacy and science. Although Tata was sympathetic, I chose to face this harassment without seeking his help. I felt proud that I had moved away from under the shadow of a giant peepul tree.

## Tata in public life: the political engagement

Much has been written about Tata's creative genius and many dimensions of his public life. Tata himself has written extensively about these events in his autobiographies.[56] Tata's political engagements that I describe here have also been filtered through the sieve of my own preferences and biases.

It is my eternal regret that Tata did not preserve any of his correspondences with historical figures like Mahatma Gandhi, Rajaji and others. Tata had visited Gandhiji's Sabarmati Ashram in his youth and consulted him on the dilemmas he faced trying to follow up on Gandhi's prescriptions for social reform. But no original correspondence exists about these milestones. Tata's routine practice was to tear up the letters he received every day, soon after he replied to them. Years later, I realised what a treasure I had lost when my colleague in WCS, Josh Ginsberg, showed me a letter from Albert Einstein he had inherited from his grandmother.

Tata had joined the freedom movement in 1922, inspired by Mahatma Gandhi. Soon he came under the spell of the tallest Congress leader in Kanara, Karnad Sadashiva Rao.

Tata once told me with great sadness how Karnad Sadashiva Rao, a man of great wealth, was reduced to penury in his final days. He was once even compelled to borrow ten rupees from his protege, Shivarama (Tata). Karnad, whose public philanthropy once knew no bounds, was unable to repay Tata before he died. Tata had tears in his eyes when he told me that story.

---

56   See B-1 to B-3 in Annotated Bibliography for more details

In his conversations with me, Tata was scathing in his criticism of some other proteges of Karnad who undercut him politically just as independence dawned. Tata was an eyewitness to their subterfuges. He blamed three Congress stalwarts in particular—Kamala Devi Chattopadhyay (herself born a Saraswat), Ullal Srinivas Mallya and K.K. Shetty. Kamala Devi is now lauded as a 'maker of modern India' for her contribution to handicrafts and handlooms and other endeavours. Mallya later became a powerful political secretary to Jawaharlal Nehru and contributed significantly to the economic development of South Kanara. Shetty groomed a new breed of street-smart Congressmen who later kept their party in power for decades in South Kanara.

In this context, I believe there is a need to lay to rest a canard circulated about Tata's wedding to Amma by the well-known Kannada journalist, late Patil Puttappa, in his memoirs.[57] Unfortunately, not only my dead parents, even my long-deceased grandfather Kamu Alva became a victim to this needless slander. Puttappa claimed that Tata had gotten Amma pregnant and had married her only because Kamu Alva had threatened to shoot him! Poor Kamu Alva, who was in declining health, and owned no gun, had committed suicide by consuming poison ten months after he had blessed my parents' wedding.

In fact, how Tata and Amma had met, and got married, has been reported in detail in their own words (chapter 2) as well as in accounts by others who were witnesses.[58]

In any case, the time lag of a year and nine months between the date of my parents' wedding and the birth of my eldest brother clearly shows that Puttappa's claim is utter nonsense. Why this ageing journalist indulged in such calumny deserves some scrutiny.

Puttappa, who lived in Hubballi, far away from Mangalore, cites as his 'source' a long-dead Congress leader who was of Tata's age

---

57   See B-37 in Annotated Bibliography for more details
58   See B-1, B-2 and B-24 in Annotated Bibliography for more details; also see chapter 2

(twenty years older to Puttappa). However, even if that Congressman did share such unfounded gossip with Puttappa, it is also worth noting that Tata had publicly blamed the same man for undercutting Karnad Sadashiva Rao.

Tata took a keen interest in national politics from his late teens. His autobiographies delve into the matter in some detail.

Initially, the radical, socialist fighter in Tata appears to have held sway. His novel *Chomana Dudi* perhaps best captures Tata's emancipatory politics.[59] It cemented Tata's reputation as a novelist, telling the story of an 'untouchable' bonded labourer whose lifetime ambition was to merely elevate his status to that of a sharecropper on leased land. Even this limited aspiration is ultimately crushed by the forces of tradition and economics that overwhelmed Choma, the main character. The last paragraph in *Chomana Dudi* is one of the most powerful, beautifully crafted pieces of prose in modern Kannada literature. Reading it sixty years later, I still find it hard to hold back my tears.

However, Tata did not remain a leftist for long. Joseph Stalin and his brutal social experiments in Soviet Russia alienated Tata from socialism in general forever.

On the international front, Tata believed that Jawaharlal Nehru's non-alignment and his dream of a socialist India were wishy-washy nonsense. Tata did believe strongly in electoral democracy in combination with a free enterprise-based economy. He argued that India should be a part of the US-led military alliances that were born after the Second World War to oppose the emergent Russia–China axis. Tata was supportive of America's misadventure in Vietnam, a position that even his favourite *Time* magazine gave up after the late 1960s.

In electoral politics, Tata was generally aligned with his eldest brother, K.R. Karanth, who had resigned as a cabinet minister in 1948 to protest the emerging corruption in the Congress party.

---

59   See B-36 in Annotated Bibliography for more details

K.R. Karanth then got involved with the Praja Socialist Party (PSP), with stalwarts like Acharya Kripalani, Ashoka Mehta and H.V. Kamath, at one point becoming the vice president of that party. Supporting his brother, Tata contested as a PSP candidate from the Puttur Assembly segment in 1952.

Amma told me a story about how, when Kripalani was addressing local voters in Hindi, which practically no one understood, the audience became restless and inattentive. Angered by this, Kripalani roared in Hindi, *'Tum Sabh Gadhe Ho!'* (You are all donkeys!) There was a moment of silence until the local interpreter caught up to sheepishly announce: *'Naavellaroo Katthegalanthe!'* (This man thinks we are all donkeys!)

In the mid-1950s, Tata endorsed the political philosophy of C. Rajagopalachari (Rajaji) who had quit the Congress party to establish the Swatantra party. The new party espoused the model of economic growth that some Southeast Asian countries were rapidly adopting. When Rajaji campaigned for the Swatantra party in South Kanara during the 1960s, Tata travelled with him, interpreting his speeches in Kannada for the voters.

When Tata was campaigning for the Swatantra party in the 1962 general elections, Amma was canvassing votes for the Jan Sangh, mainly because many of her good friends supported that party. At that time, she met a young girl, Gowri Pai, who was the sister of RSS leader Vittal Pai in Puttur. Gowri Pai (1938-) went on to become a doctor who devoted herself to social service, establishing her old-age home, Anadashrama. Gowri took tender care of Amma during some of her most difficult moments in the early 1980s. Still active in her eighties, Gowri Pai remains a cherished family friend.

Tata's attitude towards the Jan Sangh, which also endorsed the free enterprise-based economy, was more lukewarm. Tata liked the dedication and discipline of its RSS cadres and the personal honesty and integrity of its early leaders. But being an atheist, Tata could never be wholly enthusiastic about Jan Sangh's version of god's own truth.

In the 1971 parliamentary elections, Tata supported the 'Grand Alliance' consisting of the Swatantra Party, Jan Sangh, Socialists and the anti-Indira Gandhi fragments of the Congress. The electoral drubbing that Gandhi delivered to that alliance made it look anything but grand.

Indira Gandhi imposed her dictatorial national emergency in 1975. Tata was one of the few among his generation of literary intellectuals in Karnataka who boldly proclaimed his opposition. He publicly protested when many were muted by fear. Tata returned the Padma Bhushan he had received in 1968, stating that as a writer he could not tolerate a government depriving citizens of their hard-won liberties.

That was the first step in Tata's risky public stance against the Emergency. Thereafter, he became a hero to many opposition leaders like George Fernandes, Atal Behari Vajpayee and L.K. Advani, who were all either on the run or in jail during those dark days.

Tata attended anti-emergency conclaves organised by the RSS which led the fight in Karnataka, as well as similar events in Kerala organised by the Communist Party of India–Marxist (CPM). Tata would simply say, loudly and publicly, that he would vote for 'anything else, even an electric pole' if it contested against Indira Gandhi.

After the Emergency was imposed, I got interested in Marxism, appreciating Leon Trotsky's variant of that creed. Ironically, in the Indian context, I sympathised with the Stalinist CPM because I admired its leaders like E.M.S. Namboodiripad (EMS) and Jyoti Basu. I used to gently engage in conversation with Tata on these issues, but he had no time for the CPM, although he had personal regard for Namboodiripad because of their meetings during the Emergency. The only time I personally met EMS was in Mysore in the late 1970s. When I introduced myself to him, EMS remembered Tata with much regard.

At the time of Indira Gandhi's by-election bid from Chikmagalur in 1978, there was a great deal of pressure on Tata, who was then seventy-six, to contest against her. All of us in the family, including Amma, vehemently opposed the idea. Fortunately for us, a senior opposition politician, Veerendra Patil, finally agreed to contest against Indira Gandhi.

Tata at an election rally in North Kanara in 1989

Once again, in 1989, egged on by his naive 'green' friends, Tata offered a token contest against the Congress Party in the parliamentary elections from North Kanara. He, who wrote *Paraamaanu Indu Naale* extolling the promise of nuclear energy in 1955,[60] was contesting on an anti-nuclear platform! However, Tata did not seriously campaign, telling his supporters that he would be abroad during that phase. Tata, however, succeeded in siphoning away just enough votes from the opposition Janata Party, which ensured a Congress victory. I regretted that the Janata Party's candidate, Anant Nag, the actor, who was a friend of mine, had to lose as a result. Politics was something Tata jumped into periodically, took a quick dip, and got out. This 'bird-bath model' of politics did not worry me too much.

When Tata passed away in 1997, I received moving letters of

---

60 See B-39 in Annotated Bibliography for more details

condolence from many political leaders, cutting across party lines, who had met him during his brief political forays.

Among Karnataka politicians he had two lifelong admirers. One was Ramakrishna Hegde whom he had known from student days. Somewhat oddly, the other one was from the Congress—Marpadi Veerappa Moily who was inspired by Tata's emancipatory politics captured in *Chomana Dudi*. As a young lawyer, Moily had fought the landlords on behalf of sharecroppers when the land reform laws were implemented in South Kanara during the early 1970s. Both Hedge and Moily consistently supported Tata's literary and cultural efforts during their tenures as chief ministers of Karnataka.

## *Kannada pride and cultural connections*

The South Kanara that Tata grew up in was a part of the Madras Presidency. The present-day Karnataka region had been historically fragmented and administered separately by various powers.[61] Under colonial rule, the Kannada-speaking regions were partitioned among the presidencies of Madras and Bombay and the colonially supervised princely states of Hyderabad under the Nizam and Mysore under the Wodeyars. In all these units, except Mysore, the Kannada language was suppressed and Kannadigas were discriminated against in educational and employment opportunities. Consequently, there was a deep groundswell across the entire region to unify all Kannada-speaking people through 'Karnataka Ekikarana' (unification).

The idea of Ekikarana took birth in the mid-nineteenth century, building on the foundations laid by pioneers like 'Deputy' Channabasappa, Ra. Ha. Deshpande and other passionate men. The superstructure of the movement rose in the early twentieth century. The spirit of Karnataka Ekikarana was captured emotively by Huilgol Narayana Rao's aspirational song titled 'Udayavagali Namma Cheluva Kannada Nadu' (may our beautiful Kannada land rise again). It was sung melodiously at the Congress party's 39th national session at

---

61   See B-40 in Annotated Bibliography for more details

Belagavi (1924), presided over by Mahatma Gandhi. The singer was an eleven-year-old schoolgirl, Gangubai Hangal, who later attained legendary fame as a Hindustani vocalist.

Tata's love for Kannada drew inspiration from senior leaders of the Ekikarana movement like Mudaveedu Krishna Rao and Aluru Venkata Rao. Tata and his brother K.R. Karanth were both drawn into the Karnataka Ekikarana movement even before the 1930s. I think Tata's elder brother saw it as a movement for political and economic emancipation of Kannadigas, while Tata felt strongly about the cultural subjugation that Kannadigas faced, under the state-sponsored dominance of the Tamil, Marathi and Urdu linguistic minorities in all regions except the princely state of Mysore.

After Independence, K.R. Karanth was a prominent leader of the Ekikarana movement, along with his contemporaries like Ranga Rao Diwakar (a member of Jawaharlal Nehru's cabinet in Delhi). Tata aggressively canvassed for the idea of Ekikarana within his own literary and cultural domains.

Tata's pride in Kannada was not merely of the parochial kind, content to rejoice in the past glories of Karnataka. Tata was a true modernist who saw and appreciated the progress that could be achieved through science, technology and economic development. His intense belief was that Kannadigas could not be a part of such overall progress without their linguistic and cultural emancipation.

Tata's views on the unification of Karnataka were at odds with some writers of the princely Mysore state whose loyalty to the king dampened their enthusiasm for the unification. As a little boy, I witnessed the Kannada Sahitya Sammelana at Mysore in 1955, which Tata had presided over. He spoke eloquently in favour of Ekikarana to thunderous applause from Kannadigas from all over the region, muting any discordant voices.

The popular struggle for Ekikarana finally bore fruit in 1956 with the formation of the greater Mysore State (comprising of princely Mysore and other Kannada-speaking regions) which was later renamed Karnataka in 1973. The movement has been documented in several accounts, with H.S. Gopala Rao's scholarly work being the most comprehensive.[62]

The most poignant case among the votaries for the Karnataka unification was of Tata's older friend Manjeshwara Govinda Pai (1883-1963). Pai was a poet, scholar and polyglot who had been bestowed the title 'Rashtra Kavi' (national poet). Pai lived in Manjeshwara town in the taluk of Kasaragod in the South Kanara district. This taluk was unjustifiably cut off and ceded to Kerala during the formation of linguistic states. A variety of factors contributed to this injustice: the somewhat lukewarm attitude on the part of some loyalists of the Mysore king to the idea of Ekikarana being one of them.

Govinda Pai never forgave 'Sardar' Panikkar, a Malayalee member of the powerful State's Reorganisation Commission, for this injustice. Pai labelled him 'Panikkar rakshasa' (demon) and continued to insist that all letters to him should be addressed at Manjeshwara, Karnataka, and not Kerala, even if that meant Pai would not get them.

One of my little-boy memories in Govinda Pai's home is of dashing to the 'outhouse' in his coconut garden, with some urgency to relieve myself, only to come out screaming after seeing a turtle staring up from the Asian pan on which I had squatted. The great poet had to break off his passionate discussion with Tata to rescue me from that gentle, befuddled animal.

An important segment in Tata's intellectual quest was his deep interest in the popularisation of science. It was driven by a desire to make new knowledge readily accessible to Kannadigas. For him the love of Kannada and Karnataka was not just about marching in the streets, shouting slogans and glorifying the past. It was about working hard now to ensure the best ideas and things in the world reached Kannadigas most effectively.

I have tried to imbibe from Tata this kind of love for Kannada. I cannot think of myself as Indian without being a Kannadiga first.

---

62   See B-40 in Annotated Bibliography for more details

It saddens me to see so many among my relatives and friends, who admire Tata so much, have not absorbed his intense pride in his Kannada identity.

In the domain of Kannada literature, a unique aspect of Tata's status was that he never claimed to be a part of any literary movement or clique. He stayed aloof in Balavana, away from most literary skirmishes in Bangalore, Mysore and Dharwad, logging in solid ten-hour workdays, decade after decade. As a result, Tata's intellectual output is perhaps far more diverse and prodigious than that of any other Indian intellectual.[63]

However, Tata did maintain contact with his peers in the cultural world. Visitors to our home in Balavana during my boyhood included significant literary figures like Da. Ra. Bendre, K.V. Puttappa (Kuvempu), V. Seetharamaiah and G.P. Rajarathnam. Tata's many literary connections and contributions have been deeply explored elsewhere by serious scholars.[64]

## Tata's attitude to religion

Tata remained a lifelong atheist. Among Tata's generation of Kannada writers, only A.N. Murthy Rao, Gowreesha Kaikini and Rayasam Bheemasena Rao ('Ballari Beechi') were self-proclaimed atheists. Tata never reached out to god as a crutch even when facing extreme adversities in life. Amma used to read Bertrand Russell and sound like a rationalist when I was young. However, after her illnesses and Harshanna's death, she too reached out for that crutch to steady herself.

Tata placed the values of ethics and personal integrity way above self-proclaimed piety. Tata's book *Balveye Belaku* (Living the Right Way is The Only True Enlightenment) presents a brilliant exposition of his ethical atheism.[65]

---

63   See B-4 to B-10 in Annotated Bibliography for more details
64   See B-4 to B-10 in Annotated Bibliography for more details
65   See B-41 in Annotated Bibliography for more details

Tata, however, did not impose his atheism on others. In his early writings like *Devadootharu* and *Gnana*, he had lampooned Hindu gods.[66] However, later he became more tolerant of people who sought relief through a belief in god. Tata seemed to feel that if such beliefs helped them cope with their real-world problems, it was all right.

However, as Tata got older, he even tolerated some religious rituals around him to please his friends and admirers. On Tata's ninetieth birthday, I saw an amusing instance of this tolerance. Tata's good friend Mattur Krishnamurthy, a devout Brahminical theist and Sanskrit scholar, who had headed the Bharatiya Vidya Bhavan in London, had come to Saligrama to greet him. He brought along two tall, plump Brahmin priests from his village near Shivamogga. In that hamlet steeped in Vedic traditions, many reportedly speak Sanskrit as a matter of routine.

The priests had brought jagates (musical instruments) and some vibhuti (sacred ashes). Krishnamurthy first sought Tata's permission. Thereafter, the priests smeared some vibhuti on Tata, and, loudly clanging the jagates, they bellowed Sanskrit slokas. While Krishnamurthy was beaming with happiness, the bored-looking priests performed by rote. Tata stood still with a bemused look on his face. At the end of it all, Tata said he was pleased that his friend was happy.

Tata was critical of the widely-respected swamiji of Malladihalli, despite the latter's record of social service in the villages in a remote area of Karnataka. The swamiji claimed that he was a Namboodri Brahmin by birth, and was over a hundred years old, having slowed the ageing process through yoga. However, irked by these untrue claims, Tata, who knew him closely during their youth, documented the truth in his autobiographies.[67]

Tata's novel, *Jagadoddhara ... naa* (I Am The Saviour Of The

---

66   See B-14 and B-15 in Annotated Bibliography for more details
67   See B-2 and B-3 in Annotated Bibliography for more details

Universe), savagely portrays a phony godman of a type that is now all too common in India.[68]

On the other hand, many traditional swamijis have liked and respected Tata despite his atheism. The late Vishweshatheertha Swamiji of Pejawara Matha in Udupi described Tata's intellect in this way: 'As wide as the ocean to his West, and as tall as the mountains to his East.' Shivarathri Deshikendra Swamiji of Suttur Matha in Mysore is another of his admirers. When we lived in Mysore, I was surprised once to see Suttur Swamiji come to our doorsteps to drop off Tata in his car. Of course, Swamiji of Suttur is an unusual man with a wide range of interests, including wildlife conservation. Some years later, I took him radio-tracking tigers in Nagarhole!

## Tata, nature and environmentalism

Tata loved nature, animals and plants without being a specialist. His appreciation of nature had both scientific and aesthetic dimensions. Tata's interest in environmental issues emerged in the 1960s when he translated Rachel Carson's books into Kannada.

However, Tata was a technology optimist. He wrote a cogent book introducing the promise of nuclear energy and its benefits as far back as in 1955. His *Vijanana Prapancha* written in the 1960s has a full volume devoted to science and technology.

Having personally failed to sell his expensive handspun khadi to poor residents of Kanara in his youth (who preferred the cheaper and better-quality clothes from the textile mills in Manchester), Tata saw modern technology, economics and markets as necessary for social progress and human welfare. Consequently, he was critical of Mahatma Gandhi's anti-industry outlook and advocacy of cottage industries.

In his later years, while Tata continued to admire technology, he sometimes came under the sway of Luddites of various hues. His opposition to the nuclear power plant in Kaiga, in

---

68   See B-42 in Annotated Bibliography for more details

Uttara Kannada, while at the same time also opposing hydroelectric and coal-fired power generation, are examples of contradictions in his environmentalism.

Once Tata was convinced of the righteousness of any public cause, he would fearlessly fight for it. However, he was not a good judge of people, at times preferring uninformed flatterers over intelligent dissenters. These traits were sometimes misused by some crafty campaigners to draw him into supporting 'environmental causes' of dubious merit.

Tata clearly favoured industrial development and opposed Gandhian regressions of modern economics. He was in favour of advancing technologies, but in his later years opposed nuclear, coal and hydropower generation. He espoused western-style liberal democracy married to free enterprise economics but hobnobbed with socialists, the RSS and Luddites. He was an atheist who shunned obscurantism but was comfortable in the company of religiously inclined friends and swamijis. He loved his mother tongue Kannada but trawled for knowledge in the ocean of English. He lived like an ascetic but travelled the world with much passion and wanderlust. He was a tender soul who could barely watch anyone suffering for more than a minute, while being a tyrant who yelled angrily at those who disagreed with him. A democrat in theory, who was sometimes an autocrat in practice.

That was my Tata: the perennially angry man who I feared, admired and loved, all at the same time.

8

# THE INWARD JOURNEY

*Kshama Rau*

### Growing up and experiences

My earliest memories go back to when I was two or three years old. Some of these fondest memories are about Tata, who was both like a father and a mother to me. When I was sick with fever and cough, he would hug me to his chest and pat me through the night. This is something I always remember. I also recall that there was a bitter medicine that I refused to take. So Tata would put me on his lap, hold my hands and legs tight and force me to drink it. These are the bittersweet memories.

Tata was a very caring father. He was very strict too. Ullas and I were closer in age than Malakka. We were always up to some mischief or the other. Sometimes Tata would beat us up.

One such event unfolded when Ullas and I got hold of some negative film rolls of a movie that Tata had made years ago and kept in a cupboard in his study. One day Ullas and I took out all these film rolls and wound them up around his table.

Tata got very angry. He said, 'I am going to beat you.' We were terrified. Just then Amma called, 'Children, come for food,' and then he said, 'Okay, now, go, have food and come back for your beatings.'

I remember he had bought a pair of beautiful earrings for me, which I was wearing. I went crying to him, after the meal, to get the beating. He said, *'Beda, beda, bendole haakkondu attare chanda alla, hogu.'* (No, no, it is not good to cry wearing these beautiful ear tops, go away.)

Tata was very kind, but at the same time very short-tempered. People were very scared of his temper. But he also gave us much freedom to criticise, make fun of, and argue with him. There was closeness and intimacy. There was no fear in me that he was such a great man. I never thought about him that way.

Kshama and Ullas with Kallianpur Bhavanishankar Rao
and his wife Sathyavathy

I could even get angry and quarrel with him. He was very indulgent with me because I was the youngest. He used to call me Bangaru, the golden one! He would buy me some jewellery on every birthday. He had an account in Sanjeeva Shetty's cloth shop in Puttur and told me to buy whatever I wanted. I was very fond of wearing nice clothes. Most of my school friends did not have that kind of luxury. It was very special, the kind of freedom I had. I used to wonder why other people were so scared of him: perhaps because of their excessive reverence and his short temper.

When I read Poornachandra Tejaswi's biography of his father, the great poet K.V. Puttappa, titled *Annana Nenapugalu*, I see some similarities. A person who is very close to you, however great he is, will never make you feel insignificant—that attitude of saying 'you are nothing and I am great' doesn't exist. Whatever his children said, their opinion was also important to him.

Tata was always ahead of his time. His ideas were very advanced. He would try to explain to his children everything, even though we were too young to understand some of these ideas.

In 1952, Tata visited Europe, something quite extraordinary for someone like him, a writer from a small town in South Kanara. He had made the trip to study Europe's classic art galleries and museums. This was something unheard of at that time. He had even borrowed the necessary money from his friends for this crazy venture.

Amma was always worried about the family finances. Two months of travel in Europe was a very expensive venture by any stretch of the imagination—just to fulfil Tata's dream of visiting the Louvre in Paris, Uffizi in Florence and all those wonderful places. Tata travelled all over Europe mainly concentrating on visits to art galleries, museums and, of course, exploring the countryside.

I remember seeing him off at Kadur from where he took a train to Bombay to then sail by a steamship to Europe. Those are very early childhood memories.

Even when he was in India, Tata would be travelling at least ten days in a month and he would take his children along wherever he could.

He was good not only to me as a child but also to my two children, Kavya and Nishanth. He would even bathe and dress them.

If they fell ill, he would take care of them. They were very comfortable with him.

When I was a child, he used to take us from Puttur to his native village of Kota. On the way, we had to cross two rivers, at Kallianpur and Mabukala, respectively. There were no bridges. For that, we had to get into a ferry boat and cross the river to take another bus. Quite an arduous journey to take children along, but Tata liked to take us to Kota, despite these difficulties.

There was an excellent mango orchard in Balavana. Tata's elder brother, K.L. Karanth, the renowned horticulturist, had specially grafted the mango and sapota plants, as a gift to his younger brother. I have fond memories of going mango-harvesting with Tata during the fruiting season. I was around seven years old, and would run behind him with a basket. He would even climb the low branches to pull down the mangoes with a hooked bamboo pole. I would collect and carry them home. We always had a variety of mangoes to eat in Balavana.

Life was full of joys, and amusing, even though we were not very wealthy. As children, we were exposed to a wealth of experiences that were highly enriching. I can now look back, hark back, delve into that treasure trove of experiences, anytime I want.

Butterflies of many kinds were found in the Balavana woods. I also watched dragonflies with tails coloured in red and ochre. I had even named the delicate dragonfly species with canary yellowtail and greenish thorax 'Duniya' for some reason. There were wonderful birds too. The swift flying emerald dove gave us a lot of joy. So did the golden orioles, parakeets and paradise flycatchers. My brother Ullas was an avid birdwatcher even then. We also had pet dogs, cats, pigeons, even peacocks and rabbits at different times.

Tata and Amma had raised, successively, several large German Shepherd dogs which were all named after characters in Greek mythology: Helen, Hector, Bruce and Balder were some of them. At night, leopards sometimes prowled, and my eldest brother Harshanna once reported seeing a black leopard.

There was no public electricity supply in Puttur. Therefore, Tata got a diesel generator to provide electricity for our home. It would run from 6.30 p.m. to 9 p.m. The entire house was lit up as well as the stretch of road from the gate to our home. The generators made a lot of noise and this supposedly drove away the leopards. What an adventurous and brave couple Amma and Tata were!

An old lady named Deyyakku Rai, who we called 'Hotel Ajji', owned a small roadside eatery. She was a frequent visitor to Balavana. She came to milk the cows and to harvest cashew fruits and nuts when they ripened in April.

Hotel Ajji was a great storyteller. She would recount wonderful Tulu folktales to Ullas and me. She had a collection of scary ghost stories, and to hear them, we would even turn off the lights for special effects. Hotel Ajji also trained us to identify a variety of ghosts just in case we saw them. One kind would have its feet turned backwards, another would be covered in white sheets and a third variety would walk levitating a couple of feet above the ground. There were hillocks all around Balavana. On moonless nights, Ajji said that she had seen a flaming torch moving across at great speed from one hill to the next. This was the 'dondi bhoota', the torchbearer ghost!

Ajji also used to melodiously chant Tulu folk songs, such as the Paaddhanas. These tales of ancient warriors, kings and spirits are, in fact, valuable oral literature that is now rapidly getting lost.

For a long time, we had raised cows and buffaloes in a large shed behind the house. Amma used to find milk-yielding buffaloes in the villages which were on sale. We even owned a humped cow of the Sindhi breed. After a few years, villagers started selling milk to us, and our own cattle were sold off.

A few years later, for some reason, I wanted desperately to possess a cow. I pestered my parents, and finally, Tata bought a beautiful black cow with a cute little calf. I named that cow Bhagyalakshmi. I spent a lot of time in the cowshed tending to it. I learned to give it a bath, feed it and even milk it. I sometimes even cleaned the cow shed—some hands-on experience that was!

We called the hillock to the west of our house Padumale. Many times Ullas and I climbed this hill with two other kids, Girija and Sanjeeva, whose family were tenants on that property. There was a manmade, perennial water pond halfway up the hill. We wanted to find the source of the spring that fed water to the pond. This led us up to two manmade dark tunnels with knee-deep water. It was a beautiful natural spring, being cleverly harvested. We were wonderstruck. The path inside the tunnels was slippery and treacherous, but we were delighted to be there. Fortunately, our parents did not get to know what adventures we were up to.

Tata's concept of nature being the child's best school was true in our case. Most things were not consciously taught to us. We were not sent to a school until we were about ten or eleven. We only had lessons taught in the evenings for two hours, in mathematics and Kannada. The rest of the time we were free to wander around.

Tata was inspired by Maria Montessori's concept of 'play and learn'. Today it is welcomed; but at that time there were no takers. This was an experiment in which he was far ahead of his time. He started the Balavana school with very little money and faced a lot of difficulties. Nobody wanted to send their children to this school. He once told me, 'The only people I could get were orphans. They had all come from very deprived family backgrounds. That meant I had to feed them and shelter them.'

Amma was fully involved in this venture. She was managing the school as well as teaching several subjects because there were few other teachers. However, coming from such poor backgrounds, these children found it hard to cope with his education. Soon the school project ran out of money and had to be shut down.

Even after the school shut down, Tata demonstrated his Balavana experiment using us, his own children. Nature was our first teacher. Nothing was formally taught to us. We were just exposed to nature. We were free to roam around, looking for birds' nests, stare at the huge dew-laden cobwebs dangling from tall trees, the sun's rays striking them and breaking up into colours or simply walking on the dewdrops on the grass or watching a butterfly emerge from the chrysalis. We were always in search of wild pigeons and their nests, looking for their eggs. There were rolling hills all around our house. Although Balavana looked like a hill station, the weather was quite hot and humid most of the year.

Tata believed that it was very important for us to feel things with our own hands and see them with our own eyes to develop a certain kind of sensitivity. At that time, a lot of people thought that Tata was not disciplining his children enough by letting them roam around in the woods all day. From those memories of my childhood wanderings in Balavana, I later penned a poem.[69]

As an artiste, it is very easy for me now to visualise when I read Jayadeva or Kalidasa describe the creepers, flowers and the wind blowing. I can actually feel it. This is because I have experienced it so intensely in my childhood. At that time, this was not consciously taught to me. Tata had just exposed me to all these beautiful natural things. For this I must be thankful to him.

Amma and Tata taught us very good values in life: 'Chase your dreams sincerely. Whatever you want to do, don't hesitate. Be sincere about it. Never look for the outcome, name, fame or money. Go after your dreams.' Not many parents would allow that now. Amma and Tata would not find us a certain path that we were compelled to fit into—say, to be an engineer or a doctor like most parents did.

Although school education has become a little more flexible now, it is still not entirely like the way Tata envisaged it for us.

Another memory of the elders in Puttur I have is of Kallianpur Bhavanishankar Rao and his second wife Sathyavathy. She did not have children of her own and showered me with much affection right from the time I was a toddler. Ullas and I studied at the Board High School later, after Rao had retired as headmaster. Until we finished high school, we used to have lunch at Kallianpur's home close to

---

69  See Appendix 3 for the poem

the school, enjoying their refined Saraswat cuisine. Rao was a tall gentleman who meticulously tutored me in mathematics, always sharpening the pencil to a fine point and writing down the numerals neatly. The Kallianpurs were very good friends of my parents, visiting and often staying with us in Balavana. Tata and Amma helped in taking care of Rao in his final days.

The eminent botanist B.G.L. Swamy (1918-1980), son of the literary legend D.V. Gundappa, was one of our family friends. Swamy was also a fine writer and humorist in Kannada. His books on his botanical explorations, his academic life and his stance in favour of Kannada, when the culture was under threat in British India, are all memorable classics. Swamy used to drop in and chat with Tata about his work and literary issues and with Amma on philosophical issues. I interacted closely with him in Madras after I got married and settled down there.

Amma used to say that Tata chased one adventure after the other. He wrote and published his children's encyclopedia, *Bala Prapancha*, well before I was born. His next encyclopedia, *Vijnana Prapancha*, was modelled like the *Encyclopedia Britannica* and written while I was growing up. I remember that to help in this effort Tata purchased all the twenty-four volumes of the *Encyclopedia Britannica*, which arrived in large cartons. My memory of Tata's encyclopedia is that of many large cardboard cartons. Ullas and I often sat inside these cartons and played with our toys. While writing *Vijanana Prapancha*, Tata was ably assisted by Professor U.L. Achar of MGM College, Udupi. Although a very simple man, Achar was a wizard in both mathematics and physics. Achar helped Tata in translating difficult scientific concepts.

Raising the loans required for printing these massive volumes was a hard struggle for Tata. Whenever a truck arrived at Balavana laden with reams of printing paper, Amma's heart would sink. She would exclaim, 'Oh my god! Another adventure!'

In the printing press, there were giant-size shelves for stocking paper—reams of paper. Ullas and I climbed up these huge racks and played hide and seek. While playing with the workers in the press, I also learned typesetting using lead types!

These years were a struggle for Tata but he always kept us comfortable in a sort of emotional cocoon. We never felt anything was lacking. Amma faced many difficulties, but she too was prepared for them right from the time she married Tata.

Tata used to help poor people in difficulties, such as when their mud houses collapsed in heavy rain, or when a daughter had to be married off, or if someone had to undergo expensive surgery. He also wrote to politicians and public officials to assist such people in difficulties. He even filed court cases to get them justice in legal disputes.

Amma had an even stronger feeling for poor people. But Tata was concerned about everything around him. When a boy or a girl wanted to get married against the wishes of their families, Tata would stand up in support and fight with the families on behalf of these young couples. This kind of social responsibility in Tata was not confined to just people. He felt all of us should care for nature too. That attitude was not as fashionable then as it is now.

Tata would often try to explain his friend K.K. Hebbar's paintings and line drawings to me. I was initially too young to understand what was really going on. But those impressions got firmly etched in my mind as I grew older and often returned in flashbacks years later. I would suddenly realise, 'Oh, this is what Tata must have meant.'

When I was growing up, Tata used to admire European art a lot. He travelled to Europe to experience it all first-hand. He came back with many prints of original paintings he had seen: Raphael, Michelangelo, Monet and many others. These prints were displayed at our home. I grew up with them: impressionists, Renaissance artists and others. Tata would name the artists for me and explain the specialties of the paintings. Even though I was a little girl, he would still thoroughly explain these features to me.

After he returned from Europe, Tata wrote a brilliant travelogue called *Apoorva Paschima* (The Wonderful Occident).[70] When I visited Europe years later, I visited all these places.

Tata has done much in the domain of art. I was fortunate to experience all this firsthand as a child. All those pictures of great artists that hung around me gave me unique exposure to modern art at a young age.

Tata owned a Rolleicord camera that took only twelve pictures per roll. Nothing was automatic about it. He had to manually set the aperture, exposure time and focus the image. Tata taught me photography with that camera.

Tata travelled a lot. Wherever he went, he would bring back very nice children's books on birds and animals as well as storybooks. None of my friends in school or in town had them. But the kind of information Tata provided during that period was very special to me.

In Bombay, Tata had met the revolutionary, M.P.T. Acharya and his Russian wife, the famous painter Magda Nauchman, who became very good friends. Acharya had fallen sick and had returned from Germany to Bombay. Magda took care of her sick husband. She was an excellent artist. Tata told me that he would sit in her studio to watch her paint. He said she painted human beings and animals with great love and skill. Magda Nauchman had created a water colour portrait of Tata which was truly beautiful, especially the way she had captured the light in his magnetic eyes.

She also gifted Tata a large, horizontal oil on canvas painting by the name 'Diana Goes Hunting'. This picture had two naked women walking, holding two leopards on a leash, going out to hunt, in a tropical forest with papaya and other trees. This large canvas adorned Tata's library for years. He displayed it along with other paintings from the Bengal School of Art and paintings gifted to him by his friend K.K. Hebbar.

I remember Tata telling me how sad he felt because Magda had died of a cardiac arrest in 1951, just before a major exhibition of her

---

70   See B-35 in Annotated Bibliography for more details

paintings was to open in Bombay. Acharya too passed away within a year, unable to live without her.

Around the same time, Tata met K.K. Hebbar. They forged a bond of friendship and mutual admiration that lasted their entire lifetime. Hebbar later painted a portrait of Tata in a pensive mood, which was beautiful. Tata's friendship with Hebbar allowed me to visit and stay with the Hebbars in Bombay, watch him paint and explain his works and thoughts right in his studio in Bandra. A bonus from these visits was the fine vegetarian cooking of his wife, Susheela Hebbar.

In Puttur, I had no one to teach me music. However, Tata's friend and gifted musician Vasudeva Nayak from Kundapura visited us often. He taught me Hindustani music whenever he visited.

Tata taught dance to Malakka, and later, I too participated in his dance-dramas. Tata trained students of Board High School, Puttur in both dance and drama. He also organised music programmes at our home in Balavana. On some occasions, there would be a violin concert by his friend Krishammachar of All India Radio, or a Hindustani vocal concert by Vasudeva Nayak of Kundapura.

I remember writers like G.P. Rajaratnam who visited us at home. I was very fond of his song 'Bannada Tagadina Tuttoori'. The poet, Prof. V. Seetharamaiah also came and stayed with us. I admired his classy silk turban tied in the Mysore style. I did not realise that he was a famous poet at that time. When he went to bathe, Vee. See. had taken off his turban, leaving it on a table. Grabbing that opportunity, Ullas and I wore Vee. See.'s legendary turban by turns for our brief moments of glory!

There was a poignant song about a lion and a lioness in captivity by Vee. See. titled 'Mriga Shaaleya Simha Simhiiniyaru' (the lion and the lioness in a zoo). I learned that song in school. I used to cry when I read these lines: *hattadiya haddinali, suttalina sereyalli, narara ankeyoliha simha simhiharu. Malina maamsava kandu, kanneeriduttaa* (confined within just ten feet, surrounded by a cage, eating rotting meat, the lion and the lioness were crying as captives of the humans). I can still recall the images this song evoked in me. The king of the jungle sitting in a cage with a dull look in his eyes and dried tears. This song created a very profound impression on me.

On special occasions, when friends came home, Tata would read out and sing one of his geetha natakas. I remember him reading aloud *Somiya Sowbhagya* and *Yaro Andaru*. When Tata got on stage to speak, his magnetism was on full display. He could speak for an hour or more extempore and hold the audience's full attention.

On special occasions, Amma would organise for the entire family a 'beladingala oota' (dinner under moonlight). There was a large, star-shaped lily pond on our front yard. Because of water scarcity, it had been filled up to form a star-shaped platform, on which we sat in a circle for these magical moonlight dinners.

Even before I joined the Board High School, I wanted to participate in Tata's dance-dramas organised for school events. For the High School Day each year, Tata trained girls for a play he directed. When he heard I wanted to participate in these, he said, 'You are not in the school. I need to ask for permission from the headmaster.' Luckily for me, the headmaster agreed.

On getting the permission, Tata gave me a minor part in *Ruthu Yaathre*, a production on the changing of seasons. There were swans, deer and rabbits aplenty. I was given the role of a small bumblebee. There were only two bees in that play, and I was one of them. It gave me a lot of joy just appearing like a bee. For the costumes, Tata created magic with his hands by fashioning headgear with crepe paper. He designed and made the tailors stitch white crepe paper skirts for the swans. For the masks, Tata cut the paper, stuck the pieces together and painted it. And for the role of the bear, he made a bluish headgear with shiny silver foil and paint.

In another play, Tata created a life-size horse. He made a bamboo framework for the horse and wrapped it in white crepe paper. It was a splendid horse. I still remember that horse which was Rama's Ashwamedha Yajna horse, captured by his sons Lava and Kusha.

My second role was in the Chinese play, *Lady Precious Stream*, titled *Varanadi* in Kannada. My sister Malakka was in the lead role. I was to play her companion, Saki. We all wore 'Chinese' dresses. A local tailor took instructions from Tata and stitched these costumes using cloth or crepe. The rest of the costumes Tata himself prepared. My role was only to come on the stage, say my words and go backstage. However, for me, it was an important role! I forgot to go back after delivering my lines and stayed on looking at all the other wonderful characters, open-mouthed, still on the stage.

I also played another part, that of Uttara in *Keechaka – Sairandhri*. Here Arjuna, pretending to be the transgender Brahannale, taught Uttara to dance. I had auditioned with a few other girls for Uttara's part. We had to sing a few lines as a test. I suppose my singing was better than others. Tata said, 'You can do it, but you need to be stronger. I will make you eat "hatthi hindi" (cottonseed cake), which is given to cows to make them stronger.'

The kind of talent Tata had, he would create something new or change things almost every day. I held on to something he taught on one day, only to find it changed the next. It was difficult to learn under this model. That is why I began to feel that there should be proper technique and structure as part of any such training. Everything looked good when Tata performed. He emoted strongly within himself and could express it vividly the moment he heard the music, and thus created a new dance. I was just a schoolgirl of ten. I felt a strong need for structured techniques and formal training. Everybody couldn't dance like Tata! For him, it was innate. But for those who had to imitate him, there had to be a structure and framework to reproduce what he demonstrated.

All of us siblings studied in Board High School of Puttur. It was a Kannada medium, government-run school. It was an excellent school with very good, committed teachers, huge airy classrooms and laboratories with ample playground space and a wonderful library.

I decided to learn Bharatanatyam when I was about twelve and in high school. Tata did not particularly care for Bharatanatyam or any other regimented dance form where you could not include your own emotions.

Kshama studied Bharathnatyam formally while at school in Puttur

I believe whatever the medium you choose, you must put in your own emotions into it. If not, it becomes an imitation. I felt that the discipline of the body movement was necessary for me.

It could not be all impulsive like Tata wanted. However, he did tell me, 'Okay, you learn Bharatanatyam if you want to.' I joined formal Bharatanatyam classes in Puttur, under my teacher Kudkadi Vishwanatha Rai. After a few months, my dance teacher had to go to Kanchipuram to learn advanced Bharatanatyam, leading to a long break in my dancing career.

I was fond of Hindustani classical music too. Later, during my college days, I was not able to learn either music or dance. Tata and Amma had both learned Hindustani music formally for a short time at least. Tata learnt some Hindustani music from the renowned singer Sonam Singh in Mangalore. Although Tata had a rich voice, he did not train with Singh for long or with sufficient rigour to master Hindustani classical music.

Kshama and Padmanabha Rau (Babu) got married in 1971;
Tata and Amma at the wedding ceremony (Svapna on Amma's lap)

Years later, I took up dancing as a profession. I became a disciple of Guru Kelucharan Mohapatra, one of the greatest exponents of the Odissi dance form.

Kshama and Babu with Prathibha, Tata and Amma

## *Travels with Tata*

I remember travelling a lot with Tata. Even when invited to small school functions in remote, interior Karnataka, he never refused to go. When I was around, he would take me along. My children, Kavya and Nishanth, have also travelled with him extensively in interior Karnataka. Tata had an amazing memory for roads and he would always remember which way to go. We usually stayed with his friends or our hosts, rarely in hotels. No tour guide can provide this kind of exposure.

Many a time we visited K.V. Subbanna at Heggodu. At that time, Subbanna had built a splendid theatre that he named Shivarama Karantha Rangamandira. His drama group, known as Neelakanteshwara Natya Seva Sangha (Neenasam in short), had been established in 1949 by Subbanna's father and friends.

Although Tata and Subbanna never fully endorsed each other's works, they maintained a cordial relationship. I remember the wonderful hospitality of Subbanna's wife, Shailaja. In the evenings, local people interested in culture and literature would gather in a large hall in Subbanna's house for discussions with Tata. Some would also talk about their problems. Tata had these kinds of interactions constantly. I found it amazing that in such small, rural places in Karnataka, there was such interest in culture and Tata's work. We tend to think that everything innovative happens in the big city. In the small village of Heggodu, incredible cultural innovations have unfolded before my eyes. I had the opportunity and exposure to absorb so much art and culture, without being formally taught.

K.V. Subbanna later won the prestigious Ramon Magsaysay award. Neenasam, which started as an amateur theatre group over seventy years ago, has also thrived. Its theatre institute was followed by the Tirugata model of the travelling theatre repertory which is famous even today. Akshara Prakashana Publications, based in Heggodu, is now one of the major Kannada publishing houses focusing on high calibre fiction and non-fiction works. Subbanna's son, K.V. Akshara, is carrying forward the legacy of his father in an extraordinarily capable manner.

I remember once when we were driving towards Sirsi in the middle of a thick forest, Tata and I saw a beautiful peacock that crossed the road. If there was something interesting, such as animals, birds or beautiful flowers, Tata would ask the driver to stop the car. There was the fragrance of karibevu (curry leaves) permeating through the forest. Tata said those forests were full of karibevu plants. This was fascinating to me. Usually I had seen the plant only cultivated in gardens.

Although now it is fashionable to talk about conservation and ecology, at the time of my travels with Tata, most people were not even aware of the idea of admiring wild nature or walking in the forests for sheer pleasure.

Tata would recollect and share with me many such experiences of nature. Once he had come face to face with a wild tiger while hiking in the Kodachadri peak of the Western Ghats. The cat had just stood there looking at him. He was struck by its beauty and stayed still. After a few seconds, the tiger had turned and walked off. Tata's concern for nature was unique because most people around him did not care.

Another time he took me to a place in North Kanara called Bankapura, where wild peacocks were abundant. We stopped there to watch them. Nearby was the village of Laksmeshwara where there was an ancient temple. Tata, being a non-believer, was more interested in the architecture and the history of the temple than the god within.

There was one phase of his life when Tata was part of a commercial travelling theatre group, writing plays for them. He referred to them as the 'Nataka company' days. Tata recalled, 'I was here in Laksmeshwara, and I used to bathe in the temple tank. Every time I dipped and came up, my bar of soap was missing. Then I detected the thief: it was a hungry rat stealing the soap to consume its fat content!' He even made a joke of it, stating, '*Bankapurada navilu, Laksmeshwarada ili*' (the peacocks of Bankapura and the rat of Laksmeshwara).

The temples at Badami, Pattadakallu and Aihole were his favourite places. He sometimes took me there. Some structures in Aihole go back to the fourth century CE. It was fascinating also because small houses and huts were built right around these temples. Local people made free use of all these temples. They tied their cattle around the ancient temple pillars and there were holes on the floor of the temple for playing the game of 'chennemane aata' (a popular rural board game). Tata took me into some of the houses to show me how they were built mostly using wooden branches with mud plaster over cut branches on the roof. Aihole was like a nursery of varied architectural styles.

We also visited the cave temples of Badami. There were sculptures—of Narasimha and Varaha, all larger than life and stunningly beautiful. Climbing over the rock like a young man, Tata would reach the top, to the temple, very quickly. Only in the later years of his life would he tell me and my children to go up and see those sculptures by ourselves. If my two children felt too lazy to climb, Tata would order them, 'You must go up and see all these things. You must experience them while you can. I am now too old to do it.'

In Hampi, at the magnificent ruins of the Vijayanagar empire, there is a huge statue of Ugra Narasimha—one of the greatest monolithic statues we have. When the Archaeological Survey of India wanted to restore it by adding the missing limbs, Tata was very upset. Tata took up the issue seriously, all the way to the prime minister, Rajiv Gandhi, who had the restoration stopped. I thought the restoration was poor. I still remember how Tata made me sit next to the statue so that the size of the great statue could be compared to a human being for a publication of his.

Tata showed me much of the beautiful architecture of Karnataka, explaining everything in a critically aesthetic way. They are not important because they are famous pilgrimage places, but because of the art, he would insist.

Whenever we went on a holiday, Tata would insist that we go and see different places, even after he grew older and tired easily. Even in his eighties, Tata would still insist that I should take my children to places of great architecture. He had recommended that I go to Bijapur to see the wonderful Adilshahi Islamic architecture. I saw it years later, on my own.

Because I was interested in weaving and handlooms, when we were passing through the Dharwad region, he would stop at the village of Ilkal to see how its famed handloom sarees were woven.

When Tata was writing a book on the paintings of Karnataka he wanted to go and take photos of some frescos that he had not known about earlier. These were on the walls of the Narasimha Swamy temple at the village of Sibi in Tumakuru district. Tata made his own reflectors for the flashlight to take the photos. I was there with him when he took those photos at Sibi.

Tata also had a keen interest in cultural and social anthropology. While we were travelling near Yellapur in Uttara Kannada, we saw a few local people with African features. They were locally called Siddis. Tata said they had been brought from Africa as slaves by the Portuguese merchants to their colony in Goa in the eighteenth and nineteenth centuries. Some of these slaves had escaped and some others were freed. They had moved to the adjacent Uttara Kannada district and settled down there. Driving along the coast, Tata also pointed out how some women were wearing strikingly beautiful stringed beads that formed a thick roll around their necks. These women also wore their sarees with the ends tied across their necks. They were from the Halakki Vokkalu community.

Tata also had great interest in folk songs passed on from generation to generation orally. His pioneering research on the history of the spectacular folk theatre, Yakshagana Bayalata of Karnataka, is considered a landmark.

Once, while passing a village called Harigadde near Sirsi, local people invited Tata to come and see some strange pottery found in their area. Tata and I had to climb a steep hill. There were some ancient clay pots, half buried in mud. Perhaps they were a part of some ancient ritual offered to village deities. Tata later sent the pieces of pottery to an archaeologist for carbon dating, which was his practice.

Animistic worship is one of the most ancient, pre-Aryan religious practices of India. It is prevalent even today in Kanara and further south in Kerala. The 'Bhoota-Kola' or spirit worship and dances are part of the ancient, truly spectacular rituals. Tata had taken me to see the magnificent dance-drama around the legend of the famed Billava warrior spirits, the brothers Koti and Chennayya.

Around Tata's ancestral village of Kota, he and I once watched two other ancient rituals called 'Dakke Bali' and a more lavish, elaborate ritual, 'Naga Mandala'. Their dance movements are rudimentary versions of those in the more evolved folk theatre, Yakshagana. Tata said these ritual dances were likely precursors to Yakshagana. His intuitive genius and keen observations enlightened me at every step.

One of my most cherished memories is of visiting Tata with my children during the summer holidays. The train from Madras would reach Mangalore at 7 a.m. Tata would come from Saligrama to the station and stand at the exit gate of the railway platform. He would have come all the way starting early in the morning, bringing a big box full of snacks. 'Why have you brought this?' I would ask. 'I got up early and asked the cook to prepare this because the children would be hungry,' would be his response.

He gave my two children also the same kind of exposure to travel that I had enjoyed when I was young. He would take them along everywhere on what he called his 'tirugata' (wandering around). He would tell them stories every night, just the way he used to tell me. It is a pity that we did not even think of recording his tales.

Tata used to make drawings for me and Ullas when we were children, using black, red and blue ink to draw different kinds of rakshasis or animals. For Ullas, it was always a tiger that he wanted. I wanted a deer. And the stories he told at night also had to feature these animals.

My children also had these wonderful experiences with Tata. They would snuggle close to him, rest their heads on him and fall asleep, listening to his stories!

I used to leave my children with Tata during the summer holidays and go to Odisha. I would go to Guru Kelucharan Mohapatra's Gurukula and learn Odissi dancing from the maestro. I could fulfil this dream of mine only because of Tata's support in taking care of my children while I was away.

This tale of my inward journey tells me how much I owe him for what I am today.

9

# THE ARTISTIC GENIUS OF TATA

*Kshama Rau*

## *The expanding canvas of Tata's life*

Tata's life was like a vast, colourful canvas, spread over almost a century. Many were the colours of his brave saga of struggle and adventure and of his many failures and personal tragedies. Yet he dared to dream—and dream big. He bravely trod along the untrodden path, like a lone tusker, always ahead of his time. Even in the face of adverse criticism, he stuck to his guns in literature, art and environmental activism.

His rich and varied real-life experiences found expression in the classics of Kannada literature that he created. Awards and accolades and spectacular success came his way, only in his later years.

Tata created Balavana in a remote wilderness, a thick woodland on a hill slope, near Puttur in Dakshina Kannada. This was his karmabhoomi for over four decades, where the most creative part of his life was spent. It was at Balavana that his multifaceted genius found full expression. The beautiful nature which surrounded him was his muse and inspiration.

Balavana turned into a fine intellectual, cultural and literary centre of Karnataka for more than four decades. He ushered in the modernistic era, be it in literature, art, culture, environmental or social activism as far back as the early 1930s. Very soon Balavana truly became a place where a cultural renaissance was taking place. Tata's annual Nada Habba (festival of the land) attracted writers, thinkers, artists and intellectuals not only from Karnataka but outside too. As a part of Nada Habba, during the Dasara festival, Tata created dances, dramas and music in a small town like Puttur. It became such a hit that he used to get writers from outside to come and participate in the cultural events, together with the local people. His 'shanthi shibiras', 'makkala kootas', youth camps and children's camps created a great deal of interest. Karanth, the social activist, walked around Dakshina Kannada and met more than five hundred families to study their lifestyle, vocations and struggles.

His mentor, the large-hearted Molahalli Shiva Rao, stood by him and supported him in all his dreams. Tata's direct interaction with the downtrodden scheduled castes found expression in his masterpiece, *Chomana Dudi*. Many a classic followed: his simple narration, searing honesty and hard-hitting realism ushered in another wave of modernism into Kannada literature.

He held camps called 'shanthi shibira' for teachers. Tata used to interact with many school teachers to understand their living conditions. The kind of cultural anthropological surveys Tata did to understand how people lived at that time were quite unique. He went around from house to house and interviewed hundreds of people. Amma was also very much a part of this, reaching out to people in a different, more personalised manner. But Tata had a scientific bent of mind and wanted to study them. And naturally, with his keen intellect and imagination, he would write books from such real-life experiences. It did not seem contrived. It flowed out of him naturally, from the experiences he gained by meeting so many people and really trying to understand their hardships in life.

For the sake of children, he would go to different villages around Puttur, have discussions, teach drama, make artefacts with their own hands using natural materials to draw and paint. He told me that a child had brought moss from the trees and rocks and another child had made a toy bear out of that moss. Such natural creativity could be found in children.

Tata asked them to document the folk songs around that region. Then a child came up with a song, '*Chinna toogi, mai mana baagi saagi baaro bannada noole*'. It was about the weaving profession and roughly translates as 'the golden thread weaving through, with the body and mind working on it'. Children presented such stunningly interesting things when Tata was trying out his experiments.

Amma recollected how the teachers would collect a round stone from the river bank and roll it onto a flat natural slab of stone to grind coconut pulp to make a chutney to go with the simple meal of ganji (rice gruel) cooked on an open fire at the camp.

Tata conceptualised that nature would be the first school where a child could start learning. However, his Balavana method of education had to be given up in 1938 due to financial hardships, besides the lack of support from educated people who did not enrol their children. Tata's beautiful concept failed because he was way ahead of his time.

He recounted all these stories to me when I was growing up. However, Tata used to joke that he conducted his educational experiments on his own four children, adding that it did them no harm. I can say with confidence that the Balavana way of learning has greatly enriched our own lives. The joy of living and learning at Balavana has left me with many cherished memories as well.

## *Venturing into adult education*

Tata had travelled to Paris in 1952 during his trip to Europe. There he had met UNESCO's chief education officer, John Bowers. Bowers later invited Tata to the UNESCO Adult Education Camp held at the Maharaja's old hunting lodge at Ilavala near Mysore. Tata was asked to write two textbooks for adult learners. Tata, in turn, asked K.K. Hebbar to illustrate these books.

Tata was convinced that literacy books produced for children would not be suitable for adults. There had to be different stories. Therefore, he wrote two separate textbooks for an adult literacy campaign, respectively titled *Jogi Kanda Ooru* (the village that Jogi saw) and *Deva Olida Ooru* (the village that god blessed), narrating a simple tale of how villagers had recklessly cut trees and made their fields barren and fallow. When a severe drought followed, the villagers suffered. A passing jogi (mendicant) whom they sought guidance from to relieve their plight gave them a variety of seeds, advising them to plant and nurture them carefully. Over the years, the tree cover regrew, the ponds filled up and the village became prosperous again. The books had a stunning impact on readers, aided by Hebbar's brilliant line drawings.

Ullas and I were witness to this adult education camp and villagers learning to read every evening after work. But we were often distracted by a beautiful mallard duck kept as a pet by the caretaker of that lodge. We fed it grains of rice with great amusement.

Even before taking up these tasks, Tata had written a sequence of five textbooks (readers) for children, titled *Sirigannada Paathamaale*. All of us siblings learned to read Kannada from those simple but interesting textbooks. They had limericks and songs too, and photos and drawings by Tata.

While we learnt Kannada using these readers, for learning mathematics, we had another teacher. Of course, with only two hours of lessons in a day, the rest of the time we played. We were lucky, I must say. That kind of learning helped me grow as an artiste later.

One of the eminent scholars who visited us was the leading expert on dance, Sunil Kothari (1933-2020). I remained in contact with him over the years and he remembered Amma with much fondness because of her incredible hospitality he had enjoyed years earlier.

When Kothari visited us at Balavana, he was accompanied by the Zaveri sisters who were famous exponents of Manipuri dance. Tata had organised a beautiful Manipuri dance programme by the sisters in Puttur. That was when I felt strongly that I should take up classical dancing seriously. I still have my picture in Balavana with the Zaveri sisters. Years later, when I met them in Chennai, they were excited seeing this picture. 'Of course, we remember Dr Karanth very well,' they said.

## *The magic world of Yakshagana*

When I was about six or seven, I remember seeing an all-night Yakshagana performance in Kota, watching the famed artiste Haradi Rama. This is the first memory of this fantastic folk theatre form that I have. Tall and statuesque, Rama looked very much like the Arjuna whom he was portraying. This performance was in the backyard of the Hollas' Upparige Mane ancestral home in Kota. We watched it all night. Early the next morning, after that all-night performance, we ate a sumptuous breakfast of 'huli avalakki' (beaten rice soaked in yoghurt), accompanied by tasty bananas, all served on a banana leaf.

This was my first such experience and its profundity did not hit me. As I grew older and became an artiste, it was like a treasure trove that I could dip into any time.

Tata had a great aesthetic sense which I admire most. I believe he can be compared with some of India's best artistes, like Rukmini Devi Arundale and my guru, Kelucharan Mohapatra. All three had one thing in common—a very strong aesthetic sense. They also had a keen intellect and an amazing aesthetic perception of things around them.

Although these three artistes took very different career paths, there was something common in their approach to innovations: to invent, but within a traditional framework. Tata was against blindly following tradition. He was a great fan of the American dancer, Isadora Duncan. She had created her own free dance style. He had read about her life and watched a film about her. Tata wanted to create his own dance forms as she had done. The dances he taught to Amma and others in Besant School were in this mould. Tata did not want to be chained to any rigid discipline, which he said becomes imitative art. While dancing you must emote from your heart, he said.

I remember his talks recollecting his interest in the way a baby expresses its moods. For example, when it is angry, it throws out its limbs and screams; when it is sad, the baby's facial expression and movements express sadness. The baby expresses itself by using its entire body and face. What inspired Tata was this.

But as a human child grows up gradually, its movements, expressions, voice, everything gets restricted. The child is inhibited by social restrictions. Expected to behave in a certain manner, the child within the adult withdraws. When we get angry, we don't throw out our limbs. We, as adults, do not publicly display our real anger, sadness or joy. This was a very interesting idea that Tata spoke about in his lectures.

Tata adopted this basic idea in his dance-drama creations. I have watched him rehearsing. He used his entire body and his face to express his emotions just as a child would, but with an aesthetic frame and timing. It all came freely to him, spontaneously. The next day he might do something entirely different. It is not like in a classical idiom, where it is highly structured—repetitive within a framework.

As a classical dancer, I see a lot of scope within the classical framework to conduct creative experiments. However, Tata was formally not trained in any dance style. Many think he had mastered Yakshagana. But he did not train himself in Yakshagana dance. He used the concept of free expression through the entire body and face and blended it into traditional Yakshagana to create what he called Yaksharanga.

Many traditionalists were critical of his experiments for removing the speech component of Yakshagana. But overall, his model still blended well aesthetically with tradition and enriched it. It also had elements of his earlier ballet experiments. That's how an artiste who is a visionary can create something new of great beauty from traditions.

I have also seen this quality in Guru Kelucharan Mohapatra and Rukmini Devi Arundale. I have associated with them closely. They have also done highly innovative work within the framework of their dance traditions. Sometimes they too broke tradition and were criticised. But they have created works of great beauty which will endure.

The path-breaking work Tata did with Yakshagana was often misunderstood. One element was making the heavy headgear and ornaments lighter and bringing in the original traditional colour harmony back into the costumes. He also introduced spontaneous expressions without clashing with different elements. With key elements of Yakshagana, Tata stuck to the tradition such as the Oddologa dance (holding the court) and the spectacular entry of Rakshasa Vesha. In these elements, he used only the traditional footwork and movements.

Tata conducted several seminars and workshops inviting local artistes even when funds were scarce. Some local philanthropists took care of shelter and food for these camp attendees. Tata had in mind something unusual: he explored and restored many original ragas, taalas and footwork employed traditionally in Yakshagana, which had fallen into disuse. How many foot movements, how many taalas were originally there in the dance form were his key questions. To get at the bottom of this, Tata organised workshops at various places, drawing on the rich memories of older traditional artistes to resurrect the original dance form.

There was not much corporate sponsorship for arts in those days. Tata's friend and artiste Subbanna Bhat would arrange such events in Brahmavara. K.S. Haridas Bhat would organise camps in Udupi. The entire village would gather around these Yakshagana training workshops, usually held in an unused school or a wedding hall. Being very dynamic and energetic himself, Tata would drag the laggard artistes around. Sometimes he even beat them. But they did not mind because of the respectability he brought to them and their art. He made them sit down by his side like equals.

These professional Yakshagana artistes usually came from poor and educationally deprived backgrounds. They had to physically carry around all their heavy gear and costumes in large boxes made of rattan from one place to the other. The very same day they had to perform, sing and dance all through the night. They felt they were not respected by the upper social classes earlier. Tata regarded them with respect and brought them national and international exposure. Therefore, they had great love and respect for Tata, no matter what anyone else said about him or how hard he berated them during the training sessions.

Tata had outbursts of great anger, very similar to that of my own Guru Mohapatra. Even Rukmini Devi was very hard on her artistes. If they did not meet her aesthetic standards, she would fly into a rage. I think this is because these extraordinarily talented persons try to seek perfection in lines and forms. If that is not attained by the disciple, at that moment, there is a great burst of anger. At other times they are very loving people. I saw this in these three people who mentored me. They all truly cared for artistes and respected them.

Although Tata had a rich voice, he was not deeply trained in classical music. His strong point was that he could emote and pick the right raga to fit the emotion he wanted to convey. For example, he forbade playing the drums very loudly when the character on stage was expressing sadness. This ability was instinctive, not learnt. That is how he became successful with his Yakshagana experiments, even after he eliminated the speech component in order to reach the wider non-Kannada audiences.

After Tata started working with professional Yakshagana artistes, he was successful in re-training them. He could easily work with the groups of trained artistes. Before Yaksharanga, he had worked only with non-professionals, students and children. Whether it is theatre or dance, I believe you need a certain discipline over the body, mind and the voice.

Tata achieved success widely and internationally. Although some critics say he went against conventions, this move enabled

Yakshagana gain a wider audience, going as far as Japan and Italy to be appreciated by educationists, scholars and theatre professionals.

When Tata started conducting his experiments with Yakshagana, one critic had rightly called it 'a creative extension of the traditional theatre'.

When he reduced the duration of the show from all night to ninety minutes and removed all dialogue in Kannada, his work became controversial. Many traditionalists did not approve of this change. But for me, as an artiste, it made sense and made a good impact. It appeared more cohesive as it brought the different elements together much better. He also brought in some reforms in the costumes, restoring the red and gold and black combination, and making the headgear lighter. Working with traditional artisans, he created headgear which was not so heavy, without compromising on the aesthetics. Now the artistes could dance freely. And it was a lot of dance and continuous movements. He also introduced the violin to maintain some continuity. But when he took that step, again he was severely criticised locally. But he could take the art form internationally through this new format. It was greatly appreciated worldwide. The aesthetic reforms he brought into the costumes too were highly acclaimed.

At that time, 'stree veshas' (women's roles enacted by men) wore twinkling nylon sarees and all kinds of tacky plastic flowers. Tata discussed these aesthetic issues with K.K. Hebbar, who also got involved in these revivals. He sketched some beautiful drawings of how the headgear should be shaped and placed. This was before the advent of plastic. Tata then revised and recreated a lot of costumes using his natural aesthetic sense.

Tata mainly worked with the artistes of the northern style of Yakshagana called 'Badagu Thittu'. While recreating the form, he retained the traditional steps, the spectacular 'Oddologa', character entries and exit and most of the original footwork.

Tata did a lot of research to produce his major book, *Yakshagana Bayalata*. He held seminars for Bhagavathas, artistes from across

Kanara. Artistes came to Puttur to learn the new Yaksharanga format from him initially. He collected ancient palm leaf manuscripts of Yakshagana Prasangas from attics of old homes in villages to synthesise this spectacular style.

There is a very accomplished Havyaka Brahmin family of artistes, known as 'Hasyagara' (traditional comedians) at Karki village in Uttara Kannada. I still remember the patriarch of the Hasyagara clan performing the rare 'simha nritya' (lion dance) for Tata during one of his travels. Another famed family of traditional Yakshagana artistes were the Hegdes of Keremane in the same district. Even these staunch traditional Yakshagana artiste families sent their young men to learn Tata's new form of Yakshagana, which was quite a tribute to him.

Tata was upfront in calling his dance format the Yaksharanga Ballet. He never claimed it was pure traditional Yakshagana or was meant to replace the traditional form. It was a format, an innovation of his own, designed to reach a broader audience who could not understand the lengthy Kannada dialogues. This innovation won Tata the fellowship of India's national Sangeet Natak Akademi. Tata and his colleagues travelled all over the world with his Yaksharanga troupe.

Years later I met a student of theatre and dance from Italy who had come from Rome to Chennai. She told me about her meeting with a wonderful man called Karanth and his fantastic dance troupe. I was proud to tell her that man was my father. I often heard these kinds of stories from people in different parts of the world. Tata had an impact as far as Brazil, Italy and Japan.

Tata's experiments in Yakshagana were focused on its aesthetic aspects. Despite the Kannada speech part being excised, there was a continuity in the dance because of the superb choreography. Tata's experiments, in fact, restored and enriched the original music. For this, he worked with the older, traditional Bhagavathas. He got wider recognition for their art first, and awards soon followed. He also worked with charitable and governmental institutions to get these artistes old-age pensions. These old artistes would often come to him for financial help when in distress or when there was a wedding in the family. He often helped by dipping into his own pocket. Not many know about his generosity.

I believe the changes Tata introduced only enriched, and did not degrade Yakshagana as some of his critics have claimed. Therefore even traditional artistes respected him. He had a particular favourite Bhagavatha, named Januvaru Katte Srinivasa Kamath, from Mandarthi village near Kota. I too have visited his little house. Kamath was a tall man with a rich, booming voice. He was a repository of many old ragas and traditions of singing, which were on the verge of being lost when Tata began his effort to revive them.

As an artiste, now I can appreciate Tata's efforts much better. Sometimes it is necessary for someone talented like Tata to break the tradition and bring in new energy into an old art form. My guru Mahapatra also brought in a lot of changes to the Odissi dance form.

Of the many trained artistes and new students who came to study under Tata, there was a student named Sanjeeva Suvarna. He was very quick in learning and became Tata's favourite shishya. Suvarna was not a very well-known artiste initially. But he was the first to grasp whatever innovation Tata suggested. He is now the director of Yakshagana Kendra in Udupi that Tata founded with much support from K.S. Haridas Bhat, Heranje Krishna Bhat and the Pais of Manipal. A well-known traditional artiste who played warrior and royal roles, Veerabhadra Nayaka had headed that centre before Sanjeeva Suvarna.

One of Tata's famous productions was called *Bheeshma Vijaya*. In that story, Bheeshma wins over three princesses in an archery contest. But he takes a vow of celibacy and refuses to marry them. The role of the eldest daughter Ambe was played by an artiste named Dayananda Balegara. He was excellent at playing female lead roles. Tata had choreographed the scene of the three princesses playing in a lake beautifully.

Another memorable production was the one in which Sanjeeva

Suvarna played the role of Veera Abhimanyu, the young warrior. In the story, he takes blessings of his mother who cries because her little boy is going to fight great warriors. Abhimanyu says, 'Mother, my arrow is not very small. It has so much power. Though I may still be a little boy.' He goes to battle with much confidence and enters the 'chakravyuha' (labyrinth) set up by all the other warriors. Unable to come out, he gets killed by them.

Tata had choreographed this sequence so well! At the end, when Abhimanyu's body is removed, a small half screen called tere is held up to block the view. This choreography of Abhimanyu's death was a real masterstroke of Tata's because all these great warriors who see Abhimanyu dead walk backwards slowly in shame because they have killed a 'child'. This poignant scene is still so strongly etched in my memory.

Many years ago, when Tata's dance troupe came to Kalakshetra in Madras, he had not accompanied them. I asked Rukmini Devi to use the spectacular semi-circular stone stage in Kalakshetra, with the giant banyan tree as a backdrop, for the performance of Veera Abhimanyu. The dance was acted there with a few spotlights, and Rukmini Devi was fascinated by the exquisite production. All the students at Kalakshetra thronged around Sanjeeva Suvarna, who got a standing ovation!

It was a magical evening under the banyan tree. After she saw that stellar performance, any time Tata visited my home in Madras, Rukmini Devi would join us for lunch and spend time talking to him. Sanjiva has written a memorable autobiography, which includes fascinating details about the interactions between Tata and Yakshagana artistes.

Another scene I still remember is from the prasanga *Nala-Damayanthi*, in which 'Karkotaka Sarpa' (a giant cobra) bites King Nala. While wandering around under a spell cast by Shani, Nala encounters Karkotaka the snake who is engulfed in fire. Nala rescues the snake, which immediately turns around and bites him, turning the handsome king into a deformed, ugly man. Nala asks the snake,

'I tried to help you—why did you do this to me?' Karkotaka replies, 'It will help you remain hidden in the dangerous years that Shani's spell holds you in its grip.' The scene where Shani casts his spell is enacted under dim lights, as are the Karkotaka and Nala scenes—they were very powerful and dramatic. It was a very memorable performance where all traditional elements and splendour of Yakshagana were in display.

Tata was an artiste way ahead of his time. He went ahead using his judgement in all his innovations, without worrying too much about criticism or controversies. Whatever he did, he followed his own heart. Although I was very interested in Tata's experiments in Yakshagana, I did not want to participate in them. I had developed my own lifelong passion for the Odissi dance form. In my life, I have followed my own heart, as he had in his life.

## My Balavana: The vision of Karanth

The past few years have been both very rewarding and frustrating ones for me because I have become involved in the efforts of the Karnataka government to 'develop' Balavana as a fitting memorial to Tata. I am a member of an advisory committee along with Ullas and our family friend, Chiranjiv Singh.

The frustration has come about because of the overenthusiasm of local dignitaries, officials and construction contractors who are misguidedly destroying the original character of the Balavana we grew up in with intrusive and ugly landscaping and cement structures—including a swimming pool and plans for a skating rink and gymnasium! Responding to the concerns of all of us—Tata's children—the chief minister of Karnataka had set up this committee to provide oversight to the Balavana Project.

The rewarding part of the experience has been the architectural restoration of the Balavana house where we grew up. I helped curate the first lifestyle museum on Tata within that building, which was beautifully restored by the Indian National Trust for Art and Cultural Heritage (INTACH).

There are three heritage buildings in Balavana. The oldest was built around the year 1932, using only lime mortar, laterite stone pillars, wooden rafters and beams, with a Mangalore tiled roof. I spent much time with the INTACH team, comprising of C. Aravind, Meera Iyer, Sathyaprakash Varanasi and Pankaj Modi. I owe them my gratitude for fulfilling my vision. The first building is now fully restored in an architecturally scientific and aesthetic manner. Indeed, it is a befitting homage to the genius who lived and worked there.

There are two more buildings yet to be completed by INTACH. The second one is a more modern building designed by Tata with the spiral stairway leading to his study. It has a lovely view of the Birumale Hills. Restoration of this building is now partially complete. The third building is the Natya Shaale (dancing hall), which later became the printing press. When completed, this building will house the Karantha Smruthi Vastu Sangrahalaya (Karanth Memorial Museum).

These three heritage buildings are expected to be completed by the year 2023. They will thereafter be open to the public to get a panoramic view of not only the Balavana I grew up in, but also of the remarkable man whose genius blossomed there. When these activities I envision are accomplished, they will be my small tribute to my Tata.

# 10

# THE FINAL YEARS

*Ullas Karanth, Malavika Kapur, Kshama Rau*

## *From the playground to the birthplace*

After Harshanna died in 1961, Amma's physical health deteriorated. Diabetes, cancer, heart disease and neuritis—the list of her afflictions was long. She became a repository of ailments, requiring constant attention and medical care. Our relative Narayana Rao was our family doctor in Puttur. His services to Amma (and the rest of our family) will always remain in our memory.

Amma's manic-depressive illness, which tended to be dormant, started getting aggravated. She was always on the most current prescriptions of psychiatric drugs and these drugs had debilitating side effects on her physical health. Amma was in her forties and Tata in his late fifties.

Over the years, Tata did well professionally. His earnings increased as his reputation and book sales grew. He travelled a lot more, perhaps to escape the loneliness at home. As the cultural scene in Puttur faded over time, Tata's activities became more focused around Udupi.

Tata became an iconic public figure. His magnetic personality and vigour, oratory skills and incredible talent spread his fame even outside Karnataka, as evidenced by honorary doctorates that came his way from across the country, including from the Visva-Bharati University established by Rabindranath Tagore. In 1968, he received the Padma Bhushan.

Amma switched between her manic and depressive phases in cycles. In the depressive phases, she even became suicidal (chapter 5). It was heartbreaking for all of us to see her vitality crumble to dust.

In her manic phases, which lasted a couple of months typically, she would refuse to take her drugs and travel widely to visit her friends. She also became a spendthrift, giving away money to whoever asked for it.

She visited Puttaparthi to seek solace from Sathya Sai Baba, whom she knew from his early days. Ullas recalls her telling him that Baba spoke very rustic Kannada. Once Baba bluntly told her, 'You should go back and see god in your husband.' She did not like that advice.

Tata bore the burden of her illness. In the early 1970s, Tata decided he had had enough of Puttur and Balavana. He wanted to lead a quieter life closer to Udupi, where his work-related interests were primarily focused. Despite our invitations to stay with us, Tata told us clearly that he could not live in the big cities of Bangalore and Chennai, where we were living at that time.

## *Life in Saligrama*

Tata's affection for, and dependency on, Sooryanna drew him back to Kota as his final place for retirement. His elder brother K.L. Karanth's son-in-law, Chandrashekar Rao, a cheery medical doctor, lived in Saligrama village, four kilometres from Kota. Rao would help with Amma's medical problems.

When Tata's friend Ramakrishna Aithal (chapter 5) heard about his plans, he offered Tata the use of a nice bungalow in Saligrama that he was building for his eventual retirement. Aithal's offer of the bungalow was rent-free and for 'as long as' Tata lived:

all of us were very moved by Aithal's generosity. Tata, accompanied by driver Ananda and the pet mongrel Benki, moved from Puttur to Aithal's bungalow 'Suhasa' in Saligrama in January 1974.

However, Tata's unilateral decision to leave Balavana was deeply resented by Amma. Her illness at that point was in its manic phase. She decided to stay with Sooryanna and Sumathi in the ancestral house in Kota. About two months later, when she turned depressive, Ullas persuaded Amma to move into Suhasa to be with Tata.

Amma's illnesses grew over time, needing increasing medical attention. After Chandrashekar Rao passed away, Chittaranjan Shetty, a competent doctor and charming man, became the family doctor. Because Shetty took great care of Amma, Tata developed a deep affection for him and would drop into Shetty's clinic every day for a chat.

Sooryanna, whom both Tata and Amma loved like a son, was always around to help. Tata's man Friday, driver Ananda, and his wife, Pushpa, who stayed in a small cottage annexed to Suhasa, were present all the time. Rama Mogera who lived not far away assisted when called. A girl called Parvathi was employed as a cook. At Tata's request, Sooryanna found a girl (we refer to her as M) to be a typist and scribe for him.

We finally breathed a sigh of relief. In terms of the supporting infrastructure necessary, both Tata and Amma were well taken care of in Suhasa.

Ullas' wedding (chapter 5) took place in this relatively tranquil period.

Every year, on 10 October, Tata would throw a 'birthday party'—a lunch-time feast to which he invited his children, local friends and relatives. This was a sumptuous affair, superbly organised by Tata's friend Krishna Karanth from Kundapur, ably assisted by Sooryanna.

However, when Amma was in her manic phase, she made life miserable for Tata with her incessant nagging and angry tantrums.

Because of her failing health, she could no longer go off on her long trips and wanderings like earlier. She soon became obsessed only with her own needs.

Tata was getting into his mid-seventies, but still a vigorous, healthy and active man. He was getting lonely both mentally and physically. His creative abilities were waning, as we could discern from the declining quality of his writings. Tata needed someone, a woman, who would make him feel young again.

With public recognition of his genius, including his fight against the Emergency, the Jnanpith Award that came his way in 1978 and his environmental activism, Tata became a popular cultural icon across Karnataka.

Sooryanna, other relatives, friends, doctor Chittaranjan Shetty and the entire Manipal Hospital system of the Pais were at his service. Sadarame, Tata's younger brother Shivayya's daughter, also acted as his scribe and assisted in running the household for over a decade. The three of us also came over to help by turns, when Amma became seriously ill or hard to manage. We also invited Amma to come and stay with us periodically, to provide relief to Tata.

However, we could not entirely give up our professional careers and come and live in Saligrama to support our parents. Nor had Tata, who had left his parents and home in his twenties to follow his passions, done so himself. He was not willing to move away from his favoured rural scene to the big cities where the three of us lived. He understood fully well why we could not come and settle down where he had chosen to live, whether it was Puttur or Saligrama.

## A not-so-magnificent obsession

Tata's part-time scribe from 1974, M, was a diligent worker. Sooryanna thought she would serve Tata professionally without arousing Amma's anxieties or jealousies. He later told us it was his great folly.

It appears M soon realised that Tata was lonely, not a shrewd judge of character and was malleable to manipulation through flattery. He possibly dazzled M with his vitality. Addressing him as 'Tata', M gradually crept into an ostensibly daughter-like role with him. Her involvement in his household and financial affairs ratcheted up.

M came from a lower-middle-class background. She also had cases of mental illness running through her family. She appeared to have realised that Tata had offered her a way out of her difficult situation. Perhaps she spotted an opportunity for public recognition riding on his fame and intellectual capital.

Amma watched all these events unfold sadly, but did not react when she was in the depressive phase. When her mood swung into the manic phase, Tata found her verbal attacks unbearable.

By the early 1980s, M was travelling around with Tata and their relationship had become an object of crude gossip in their rustic environment.

Others noticed this change too. Vasantha Sathyashankar, who was a friend of both Amma and Tata from the 1930s, joked with Ullas, 'Your Tata is in some sort of calf-love with that silly girl.' All of us noticed a distinct coyness in Tata's tenor as he incessantly praised M for her supposed talents.

Around 1981, Amma had a major fight with Tata about M. She came and stayed in Mysore with Ullas for a few months. When she slid back into depression, Amma returned to Saligrama. She found M entrenched even more firmly in Tata's life.

Tata's dependence on M gradually turned into a singular obsession.

Driver Ananda had ferried Tata around wherever he travelled, for twenty-two long years. Because Ananda was privy to every detail of Tata's daily life, he became an inconvenient presence at this point. Because Ananda had been 'like a son'—in Tata's own words—he was trusted and respected by the whole network of Tata's relatives and friends.

However, M managed to convince Tata to get rid of Ananda. Ramakrishna Aithal, Ullas and Kshama, among others, tried hard to convince Tata to change his mind. However, none of this worked and Tata terminated Ananda's services.

We were shocked and saddened by Ananda's departure.

However, Tata did make some provision in his will for some financial support to Ananda. Even after he fired Ananda, Tata tried, but failed, to get a plot of government land allotted to him. Tata hid these efforts from M, perhaps to avoid her tantrums.

M soon appeared to ratchet up the psychological pressure on Tata. She professed that she now wanted to get married, so that her younger siblings could follow as the tradition demanded. She located a US-based groom from her own community. Their wedding took place in Saligrama with Tata present as an honoured guest. He also made sure that Amma attended the wedding. Amma told us later that she felt slighted at the ceremony.

M and her husband had left for Bombay after the wedding, supposedly enroute to the US. Only the groom reached America. Within a couple of weeks, M was back in Saligrama. That was the last anyone heard about her marriage. She had demonstrated her emotional stranglehold over Tata. He could be made to get her married off, as well as to welcome her back within a few weeks. During her absence Tata had visited Mysore. He confessed to Prathibha how forlorn he felt in her absence, while still carefully portraying his relationship with M as a purely platonic one.

After multiple illnesses, Amma finally passed away on 23 September 1986 at the age of 67. She was cremated in the garden around Suhasa, now lush with palm trees thanks to Ananda's diligent care over the decades. As we remember vividly, as soon as Amma's cremation ended, Tata went upstairs to his desk in Suhasa. At that moment, M engaged him in an animated conversation about her new hobby, 'bird-watching'! We were all quite taken aback by how casually Tata had moved away from Amma's death.

Ullas was surprised when Tata wrote to him that M had re-discovered a near-extinct bird species called the Jerdon's Cursor near Saligrama. This species is a holy grail for Indian birders. Aware that only a few birds remained in the dry scrub forests near Kurnool in Andhra Pradesh, Ullas was skeptical about its 'discovery' by M in the rainy Kanara coast. Tata dashed around with M trying to photograph the bird to prove M's discovery. The bird in the photo turned out to be a common red-wattled lapwing, nicknamed in English as the 'Did you do it' bird for its peculiar call. Tata had been clearly bowled over by M and her ever-expanding suite of talents!

On 8 February 1988, Sooryanna died when a rashly-driven speeding taxi rammed into his scooter. This was a huge shock to us all, including Tata. Sooryanna's death removed from the scene someone dependable, in whom Tata had much trust and affection.

As his children, knowing about his loneliness and problems with Amma, we would have had no problem if Tata had found some decent woman to share the last few years of his life with. Our anxiety was about the mindset of the individual about whom he was becoming obsessed.

We were fully aware that Tata had helped her to acquire a plot of land, to deal with its associated problems and to build a house on the plot. He had also assisted her to get a college degree remotely and thereafter obtain a decent job. He intervened to help her whenever she faced any problem.

Our worry was simple. We detected a behaviour pattern in M of trying to establish her monopoly over Tata's affection, by making him get rid of all the trusted individuals who had stood by him for years. For such a person, we felt, a monopoly over Tata's affection, proximity, material assets and intellectual property would be the goal.

However, M's public image had to be cast as one of a doting 'adopted daughter' as well as a capable intellectual inheritor.

All three of us did share our opinion about M with Tata frankly. When Kshama cautioned Tata about their relationship, he thundered that no one in the world could change his ways.

Tata liked to visit Ullas in Mysore. However, Ullas told Tata that M was not welcome into his home. Although Tata found another place to stay in Mysore when she was with him, he continued to visit Ullas when he came alone.

It appeared Tata was being torn between his affection for us and his obsession with M. He clearly wanted us to approve of his relationship with her. However, the mental agony that M had inflicted on Amma and others loyal to Tata, had turned us cold towards her.

## *The estrangement*

On 2 February 1993, Ramakrishna Aithal, Tata's friend and benefactor who owned the Suhasa bungalow, died of a cardiac arrest. Concerned that his family would want the bungalow back, Tata contemplated moving out. Just to ensure that there was a backup plan if that contingency arose, Ullas visited Saligrama to meet Sooryanna's wife, Sumathi. Ullas asked Sumathi if Tata could stay in the ancestral house in Kota. Sumathi, who was fond of Tata and was staying alone in that large house, was happy with the suggestion. When Ullas explained the backup plan to Tata, he too agreed readily.

However, there appeared to be no urgency for Tata to move out right away because Aithal's family had not asked for the possession of the house.

Meanwhile, local gossip about Tata and M had been getting nastier after M had abandoned her husband and returned to Tata. An anonymous letter addressed to M, but circulated widely, attacked M viciously. It claimed to be from a woman who wished her well. Although written in a crude, rustic style, the letter did reveal some awkward facts. For instance, it pointed out that even as M claimed she was taking care of Tata, she had abandoned her own sick mother to someone else's care.

Tata took this nasty letter to heart. He even believed M's absurd suggestion that Malavika was its anonymous author. Tata never shared this allegation with Malavika, who eventually heard it from a cousin in distant Belagavi. The usually docile Malavika immediately rushed to Saligrama and confronted Tata about this allegation. Tata claimed that M had got an 'expert' to testify that Malavika's handwriting matched that on the anonymous letter. Malavika easily demonstrated that the handwriting was nothing like hers. She also angrily pointed out that she did not speak or write in the Kundapura dialect used by the letter-writer. Tata finally came to his senses and backed off from his allegation. However, he felt the need to pin the blame on someone.

Dr Chittaranjan Shetty had, for years, taken care of Tata's health as well as that of Amma's while she lived. M appeared to have picked him up as the next scapegoat. According to Tata's old friend Ganesh Bhat, who lived near Udupi, Tata had suddenly come to believe M's recent opinion that Shetty was an incompetent doctor because he was trained in an academically inferior medical college. When Bhat fact-checked, he found that Shetty had studied in a different college. Bhat was also upset to find that, based on M's opinions, Tata was even suspecting the medical competence of Malavika's husband, Ravi. He felt Tata was gradually turning hostile towards his own family members.

Admirers and friends who stood by Tata: Dr Chittaranjan Shetty and Prof. Ganesh Bhat

Just six months earlier Tata had spoken to us with concern about Chittaranjan Shetty's own ill-health. Now he chose to foist the responsibility of the anonymous letter on the poor doctor and cut off all contact with him.

Ullas intervened to defend Shetty, to whom we were all grateful for his years of assistance to our parents. In his response letter dated 9 May 1993 to Ullas, Tata alleged that M had suffered deeply because all three of us appeared to have joined forces with the local malcontents to discredit her. He said there was no need for any of us to 'investigate the matter' of the anonymous letter any further. He went on to say this campaign against M was a wildfire 'ignited' by Amma while she was alive.

In June 1993, Ullas went off to the US on a work-related trip of over a month.

While Ullas was away, one of Tata's friends told him that Aithal's family was in financial distress and wanted to sell the Suhasa property. And since Aithal had given Tata a 'lifetime tenure', they were in a dilemma. (Whatever the truth of this story was, the house was sold by the Aithal family only after three more years had passed.)

This intervention by Tata's nosey-parker friend appears to have provided M an opportunity to derail the earlier plan of Tata moving to the Karanth ancestral home in Kota. Tata informed Prathibha that he was making alternate arrangements for his residence. On hearing this, Ullas sent a fax from the US to Tata, inviting him to stay in Mysore with him.

Tata informed Prathibha that he was adding more space to M's house and would move in there. He mentioned Ullas' 'generous offer' but said he had made up his mind. He had already substantially funded M's home improvements and used his influence to deal with her property disputes. He was even running errands for her such as paying her electricity bills and collecting cooking gas cylinders. Tata moved into M's home by the end of July 1993.

Over the years, key individuals whom Tata had trusted for years had all been alienated and distanced from him under one excuse or the other, including Haridas Bhat in 1982, Ananda in 1986, Chittaranjan Shetty in 1993, our cousin Sadarame in 1996 and several others. Amma had died in 1986 and Sooryanna in 1988.

In their place, M was now Tata's sole window to the world and his gatekeeper.

However, the underlying reason for M isolating Tata from other trusted individuals with access to him became obvious to us later in 1996, when Tata sent Ullas a copy of his third and final will. He had executed this will two years and five months earlier, on 18 June 1994. However, he had not immediately shared the latest will with Ullas, unlike in the case of his earlier ones.

Right from the beginning Tata had appointed Ullas as the executor of wills, including the last one. The first of these wills was made in 1982, and later modified by three codicils he added in 1983, 1985 and 1987 respectively. His second will was made on 2 May 1992.

Until Tata moved in with M, he had retained two key features in all his wills. First, Kshama was to be the residuary legatee for all undesignated assets and incomes that accrued. Second, Tata had specified that copyrights to his creative works and related professional incomes should be managed only by Ullas, and used solely to support public causes. In his first will of 1982, Tata had expressed a desire that Ullas should set up a charitable trust for the purpose.

In the codicil Tata added in 1985, after Ullas had set up a trust to support wildlife conservation titled Centre for Wildlife Studies (CWS) in 1984, Tata had assigned his copyrights and related incomes to CWS. Prathibha's father Sarvotham Shetty and Ullas's friend Ajith Vombatkere were the other two trustees of CWS. One thousand rupees donated by Tata was the foundational contribution to the CWS trust.

In the 1992 version of his will, Tata mentioned that he had received a corpus fund of Rs 1,34,000 collected by his admirers, which he was using to support public causes. He specified that all copyright and related incomes described in his will should also be merged with this existing corpus fund and should be managed by Ullas for public charitable purposes.

In these wills Tata had made some financial provisions for driver Ananda and some others who had helped him over the years. There was no mention of M or any services she rendered to Tata in any of these wills. Nor was there any provision for M in his wills or codicils up to June 1994.

However, within ten months of moving in with M, Tata executed his final will. There were two major changes. Kshama had been removed from her position as his residuary legatee for any unallocated assets and incomes, and had been replaced by M. For managing the trust funds held for charitable purposes, as well as the copyright to his works, Ullas was replaced by M.

Although Tata made no mention of M's services from 1974 in any of his earlier wills, in his third will he was full of effusive praise for services that she had rendered. He also waxed eloquent about her stellar qualities as a promoter of his creative works. To her credit, M did prepare useful compendiums of all of Tata's works.

Going a step further, straying far away from the truth, in this new will Tata praised M for nursing Amma through her long periods of illness until her death.

Ullas immediately shared this latest will with Malavika and Kshama.

Ullas also wrote to Tata on 2 November 1996, stating, 'Your money, accomplishments and fame are your own, and I completely and wholeheartedly agree with whatever decision you may take in this regard.' He then went on to say, 'You have given me, Malakka and Kshama, in ample measure, the affection, education and security we needed. Based on this foundation we have all achieved substantial successes in our own professional and personal lives, without using or misusing your name.'

However, Ullas took exception to the new text in the will Tata had added to praise M as someone who had taken care of and nursed Amma through her prolonged illnesses. He wrote: 'However, I must disagree with one completely unnecessary statement which you have made in your will (and which you had earlier made in the latest version of your autobiography). This is the untrue statement that M looked after Amma in her illness. Amma, before she became ill in the 1960s, was a major force behind your early accomplishments. She toiled hard to maintain Balavana, and was a source of affection to us and others. When she became mentally ill, she became a terrible burden on all others around her, and, I know you bore the brunt of her irrational behavior. From then on, until her death in 1986, the persons who served her with affection under most trying circumstances include Rama, Cecilia, Ananda, Parvathi and other servants and Sooryanna and Sumathi. The three of us (Mala, Kshama and me) and our spouses helped when we could. Dr. Gowri Pai and Dr. Chittaranjan Shetty were the two doctors who cared for her deeply and treated her never-ending complaints. Amma did not like M, and in fact, for several years, kept her out of Suhasa. This part of her life history when she was sick is as important to her children as the earlier part when she was well and a wonderful mother. Therefore, I am copying this letter to Malakka and Kshama. The truth about who really cared for our mother cannot be changed by any rewriting of her life's story by you or anyone else. I am sorry if I have hurt you with my plain speaking. It is a trait I have inherited from both my parents.'

Ullas concluded his letter with a prosaic footnote conveying his good wishes.

In response, Ullas got a two-page, angry handwritten missive in Kannada. The missive reiterated his earlier accusation that the three of us had denigrated M because our minds had been poisoned by others. He wrote that he was a personal witness to how deeply M had cared for Amma and had nursed her through her illness.

We dropped the matter at that, not wanting to agitate him further. The truth was, Amma had detested M, and sarcastically referred to her as 'Malina' (the impure one).

Tata's anger at us cooled off after a while. He perhaps realised we were not interested in arguing with him about the material changes he had made in his final will.

Even after Tata moved into M's house, we maintained contact with him. We visited him once or twice a year. However, we stayed with Sumathi in the ancestral house. He too visited our homes occasionally. However, our relationship with him was certainly not as warm as earlier.

It also appeared to us that Tata was losing his memory. In his last autobiographical account,[71] Tata's account of Amma's attempted suicide is quite at odds with the factual narrative that Rama Mogera, who had saved her life, shared with us (chapter 6). Clearly Tata was no longer entirely who he used to be. He often only signed the letters that were supposedly written by him.

In August 1997, just before Krithi left for her studies in the US, Ullas and Prathibha took her to see her beloved 'Tatajja'. Tata corresponded regularly with Prathibha; his letters sometimes had a drawing or a joke for Krithi. They had a pleasant visit with him.

10 October 1997 was Tata's ninety-fifth birthday. M and other locals had organised a celebration at her home for him and Tata had invited all of us over. The three of us and Prathibha had gone there from Bangalore. We stayed in the Kota house, but spent most of the day with Tata at M's house. We were cordial to her, and Tata seemed genuinely pleased. We did not realise that this would be the last time we would ever see him alive.

We did feel sad to see Tata's routine in that dingy house in the middle of a crowded street in a small town. M cooked all the food for the day and left it on his table when she left for work. The Epicurean, who used to eat only freshly-cooked food for every meal now ate stale food uncomplainingly. He only seemed to crave the endless flattery and attention she provided.

This was his choice. We stayed out of it all, although our relationships with M continued to be strained. Ullas spoke to her

---

71   See B-3 in Annotated Bibliography for more details

minimally when necessary and Kshama and Malavika did not attempt to communicate with her.

## Back to the ocean

Tata had come to Bangalore by air on 27 November 1997 on some work and stayed in Anandarama Holla's Hotel Janardhana for two nights. He flew back to Mangalore on 29 November, dropping in on our cousin Shyam Sunder and chatting pleasantly with him for a while before heading to the airport. Tata smilingly turned down Shyam Sunder's suggestion that he stay on in Bangalore with him since he had to come back to Bangalore again in a couple of days for work.

However, we heard later that when Tata landed at Mangalore airport, he fell down. Tata seemed to have been feeling weak after his return to Saligrama, suffering from a viral fever as well as an ear infection. He was admitted to Manipal Hospital on 2 December, but continued to be active, chatting and joking with the hospital staff and doctors. On 3 December, a contingent of his fans and reporters from the newspaper *Udayavani* visited him at the hospital. He spoke to them animatedly. His visitors also included Heranje Krishna Bhat of MGM College and the noted Yakshagana drummer, Hiriyadka Gopala Rao. A photo in the *Udayavani* newspaper the next day captured that event. This is probably the last picture of Tata in a conscious state.

The next day, on 4 December, we heard for the first time that Tata had suffered a stroke and was in the ICU in Manipal Hospital. Ullas and Malavika hired a taxi and drove through the night to reach Manipal early in the morning of 5 December. Tata was unconscious, with his silver-white mane spread on the pillow, forming a halo around his head. Someone remarked that he looked like a sleeping lion!

Having heard the news from a forester colleague who was a fan of Tata, Shyam Sunder too had driven with him through the night to reach Manipal to see his beloved Shivarama Mava.

The next day Kshama, her husband Babu and daughter Kavya, along with Ravi and Prathibha flew to Mangalore to join Ullas and Malavika at the hospital. However, Tata continued to be unconscious, and was on a ventilator throughout. He finally passed away on 9 December 1997 at 11.35 a.m. The clinical cause of death was 'renal failure, septicemia and acidosis'.

Through the night of 9 December, Tata's body lay in state at the Giliyaru Shaale founded by his father. Next morning Tata was cremated in the back garden of the ancestral Karanth house at Kota, which belonged to the family of Sooryanna, whom both our parents had considered to be their own son.

We were overwhelmed by the public response to Tata's death. The dignitaries who visited him in the hospital, the crowds that thronged to Kota for his state-sponsored ceremonial funeral, personal messages and letters of condolence pouring in from the high and mighty—including Prime Minister Vajpayee and Home Minister Advani—as well as from hundreds of his fans from across India. Eloquent tributes flowed in the popular media, in English, Kannada and other Indian languages.

Tata, the lifelong atheist, had directed in his will that no religious obsequies be performed for him. Some of our cousins conducted a Brahminical shraddha for him. Although we did not participate, we did understand their compulsions of tradition.

Kshama and Malavika quietly took Tata's ashes to the beach in Kota for immersion in the sea. The Skanda Purana has it that Parashurama (Bhargava) had flung his mighty axe as far as he could, ordering the ocean to retreat, to create this beautiful land in which Tata was born. Tata, who was popularly known as Kadala Teerada Bhargava (Parashurama of the ocean shore), had finally returned to that ocean.

These were all stark reminders to us that, as far as people were concerned, Kota Shivarama Karanth was their property. We had an obligation to share our 'Tata' with all of them. However, 'growing up Karanth' was a uniquely personal experience to each one of us. No one else could claim that rare privilege.

# ANNOTATED BIBLIOGRAPHY


**B-1**.  K. Shivarama Karanth, *Huchhu Manasina Hatthu Mukhagalu [Ten Faces of a Whimsical Mind]* (Harsha Prakatanalaya, Puttur, 1948). A chronological autobiography and this edition was followed by several subsequent revised editions between 1948 and 1995 during his lifetime by various publishers.

**B-2**.  K. Shivarama Karanth, *Smrithi Pataladinda [Memories on the Screen]* (Rajalakshmi Prakashana, Bangalore, 1977, 1978, 1979). A thematically separated autobiography in three volumes.

**B-3**.  K. Shivarama Karanth, *Alidulida Nenapugalu [Fragments of My Memory]* (SBS Publishers & Distributors, Bangalore, 1995).

**B-4**.  C.N. Ramachandran, *K. Shivarama Karanth*, 'Makers of Indian Literature' (Central Sahitya Academy, New Delhi, 2001, 2008). A monograph in English.

**B-5**.  Ramachandra Guha, 'The Kannada Tagore' (*The Telegraph*, Calcutta, 14 October 2002) and 'In the Presence of Greatness' (*The Telegraph*, Calcutta, 25 January 2014).

**B-6**.  M. Malini Mallya (ed.), *Shivarama Karanthara Krithi Kaipidi [A Comprehensive Compendium of Shivarama Karanth's Works]* (Rashtrakavi Govinda Pai Research Centre, MGM College, Udupi, Karnataka,1997).

**B-7**.   T.P. Ashoka, *Shivarama Kararantha: Yeradu Adhyanagalu [Shivarama Karanth: Two Studies]* (Akshara Prakashana, Sagara, Karnataka, 1992–2015). A literary commentary published in six editions.

**B-8**.   Jayaprakash Mavinakuli (ed.), *Karantha Yugantha [End of the Karanth Era]* (Shivarama Karanth Study Centre, Vivekananda College, Puttur, 1999). A compilation of 89 articles in Kannada, 11 articles in English and four appendices on Tata's works.

**B-9**.   Jayaprakash Mavinakuli (ed.), *Neranudige Nooru Varushagalu [Speaking Straight from the Heart Through an Entire Century]* (Sahitya Prakashana, Hubballi, Karnataka, 2005). A compilation of 39 articles in Kannada about Karanth.

**B-10**.   Eshwara Bhat Bolanthakody (ed.), *Abhimana [Pride]* (Puttur, Karnataka, 1992). A collection of 86 articles in Kannada by various authors on Karanth's work and legacy and about several significant writers, intellectuals, artists, social workers, political and religious leaders of Kanara, published as a volume to commemorate the Fifth Kannada Literary Meet of South Kanara District.

**B-11**.   Naga Aithal (ed.), *Karantha Chinthana [Thinking about Karanth]* (Akshara Prakashana, Sagara, Karnataka, 2000). A compilation of 26 articles in Kannada about Shivarama Karanth by Kannadigas settled abroad, with a foreword by U.R. Ananthamurthy.

**B-12**.   K. Shivarama Karanth, *Marali Mannige [Return to the Homeland]*, 1941. Novel.

**B-13**.   K. Shivarama Karanth, *Halliya Hatthu Samastharu [Ten Respectable Persons in the Village]*, 1944. Satire.

**B-14**.   K. Shivarama Karanth, *Devadootharu [God's Messengers]*, 1924. Satire.

**B-15.** K. Shivarama Karanth, *Gnana [Deep Knowledge]*, 1935. Satire.

**B-16.** G. Vasudeva Herle, *Keerthishesha Kota Shesha Karantharu: Jeevana Smarane [Life and Memories of Kota Shesha Karanth]* (Board and Teachers of Giliyaru Shaale, Kota, Karnataka, 2008). A commemorative illustrated booklet in Kannada.

**B-17.** S.N. Malla and K.S. Upadhya (eds), *Kota Ramakrishna Karantha Smaranasanchike* (Mangalore, 1985). A commemorative volume on K.R. Karanth, with 25 articles in Kannada and 4 in English.

**B-18.** Vaidehi, *Nenapinangaladalli Mussanjeya Samaya* (Manohara Grantha Mala, Dharwad, 2015). A biography of K.L. Karanth.

**B-19.** B. Surendra Rao, *Bunts in History and Culture* (MGM College, Udupi and the World Bunts Foundation Trust, Mangalore, 2010). A scholarly book about the Bunt community.

**B-20.** Frank F. Conlon, *A Caste in a Changing World: Chitrapur Saraswath Brahmins: 1700-1935* (The Center for South and Southeast Asian Studies, University of California, Berkeley, USA, 2002). A scholarly monograph.

**B-21.** K. Shivarama Karanth, *Audaryada Urulalli [In the Noose of One's Own Generosity]*, 1947. Novel.

**B-22.** Padukone Prabhashankar Rao, *Nenapugalu: Telibanda Yelegalu [Leaves That Floated By: A Memoir]* (Manohara Grantha Mala, Dharwad, 2016).

**B-23.** Manorama M. Bhat (ed.), *Dakshina Kannada Jilleya Modala Lekhakiyaru [Early Women Writers of South Kanara District]* (Karavali Lekhakiyara-Vachakiyara Sangha, Urva Store, Mangalore, 1996). A collection of 13 articles in Kannada.

**B-24.** B. Leela Bhat (ed.), *Leela Karantha Nenapina Samputa [Leela Karanth Commemorative Volume]* (Shivarama Karanth Study Centre, Vivekananda College, Puttur, Karnataka, 2001). A compilation of nine articles in Kannada and two in English as well as nine Kannada poems and a collection of personal correspondences of Leela Karanth.

**B-25.** Narayana Manjeshwara, *Karantharondige Kelavu Varshagalu [Some Years with Karanth]* (Navakarnataka Publications, Bengaluru, 2005). A personal account in Kannada about the author's life with the Karanth family in Balavana.

**B-26.** Rekha Bannadi, *Leela Karantha* (Sapna Book House, Bengaluru, 2008). A short biography of Leela Karanth in Kannada.

**B-27.** K. Shivarama Karanth, *Bala Prapancha*, 1936. A children's encyclopaedia in 3 volumes.

**B-28.** K. Shivarama Karanth, *Vijnana Prapancha*, 1959–1964. A science encyclopaedia in 4 volumes.

**B-29.** K. Shivarama Karanth and Leela Karanth, *Yaaru Lakshisuvaru?* [Kannada translation of Marathi novel *Pun Lakshath Kon Ghe To? (But Who Cares?)* by Harinarayan Apte], 1951.

**B-30.** K. Shivarama Karanth, *Sameekshe [The Overview]*, 1956. Novel.

**B-31.** G.M. Carstairs and R.L. Kapur, *The Great Universe of Kota* (University of California Press, Berkeley, USA, 1976).

**B-32.** K. Shivarama Karanth, *Kota Mahajagatthu* [Kannada Translation of B-31], 1985.

**B-33.** Kanak Chandra Deka (ed.), *B.K. Bhandari, Smrithigrantha* (Nayana Bhandari Sharma, Guwahati, Assam, 1997). A commemorative collection of articles in Assamese and

English, including one in English by Shivarama Karanth on the life of B. Kochanna Bhandari.

**B-34.** K. Shivarama Karanth, *Bettada Jeeva [Man from the Mountain]*, 1943. Novel.

**B-35.** K. Shivarama Karanth, *Apoorva Paschima [The Wonderful Occident]*, 1954. Travelogue.

**B-36.** K. Shivarama Karanth, *Chomana Dudi*, 1933. Novel.

**B-37.** Ananda Poojari, 'Naa Kanda Karantharu' *[Karanth in My View]* Article in Kannada magazine *Taranga* dated 13-12-2001.

**B-38.** Patil Puttappa, *Naanu Pateela Puttappa* (Lohiya Prakashana, Ballari), Volume 1. An authorised biography narrated by Sarjoo Katkar.

**B-39.** K. Shivarama Karanth, *Parmanu, Indu Naale*, 1957. A Kannada translation of Margaret O' Hyde's *Atoms Today and Tomorrow*.

**B-40.** H.S. Gopala Rao, *Karnataka Ekikarana Ithihasa [A History of the Unification of Karnataka]* (Navakarnataka Publications, Bengaluru, 1996-2018). A scholarly book on the socio-cultural, historical and political movements covering the formation of the Kannada identity and re-unification of Karnataka.

**B-41.** K. Shivarama Karanth, *Balveye Belaku* (Living the Right Way is the Only True Enlightenment), 1950. Philosophical treatise.

**B-42.** K. Shivarma Karanth, *Jagadoddhara … na [I Am the Saviour of the Universe]*, 1960. Satire.

**B-43.** K. Shivarama Karanth, *Jogi Kanda Ooru [The Village That Jogi Saw]*, 1954. Textbook for adult literacy.

**B-44.**   K. Shivarama Karanth, *Deva Olida Ooru [The Village That God Blessed]*, 1954. Textbook for adult literacy.

**B-45.**   K. Shivarama Karanth, *Sirigannda Pathamaale*, 1941. Readers for primary school, classes 1 to 5.

**B-46.**   K. Shivarama Karanth, *Yakshagana Bayalata*, 1963. A scholarly book on the Yakshagana folk theatre.

# APPENDIX–1

# KOTA SHIVARAMA KARANTH: A PROFILE

Shivarama Karanth (1902–97) was born in an orthodox Brahmin family in Kota village in the South Kanara district of Karnataka. He was first schooled in his village and later in the Kundapura High School. Karanth was deeply influenced by Tagore and other Bengal intellectuals as well as by his mentors in Karnataka. As an idealistic student in Mangalore, Karanth was inspired by Mahatma Gandhi to quit college to join the freedom struggle. Through the 1920s and early 30s, he tirelessly followed the Gandhian path, undergoing incredible personal hardships. However, by the 1930s, disillusioned by Gandhi's ideologies, Karanth shifted his focus to achieving pragmatic social reforms. He also nurtured his burgeoning talents in journalism, creative writing, the performing arts, popular science and children's education.

Karanth settled down near Puttur in South Kanara to establish his creative base at Balavana. In 1936, Karanth's inter-caste marriage to Leela Alva raised a storm among conservative social forces in Kanara. For the next four decades, Balavana became the crucible of his creative work in multiple domains.

Karanth's prodigious intellectual output includes 45 novels, 31 plays, 6 travelogues, 6 satires, 231 tracts of children's literature,

9 philosophical tracts, 8 books targeting adult literacy, 13 books on fine arts, 9 autobiographical writings, including two full length volumes, 1 Kannada dictionary, 17 popular science books, including two encyclopaedias, 5 edited books, 16 translated books, 4 short story collections, 2 poems and 108 articles—all in Kannada. He also wrote 7 articles in English.

In his professional career, Karanth also dabbled in journalism, movie-making, running a printing and publishing house and campaigning for environmental and political causes. He even contested in the elections twice, and lost.

Through much of this productive creative career, Karanth was unflinchingly supported by his wife Leela Karanth (1919–1986). During his career, several seniors, mentors, peers and admirers as well as subalterns assisted the blossoming of Karanth's genius.

The Karanths had four children, the eldest being Harsha who died in 1961, followed by Malavika, Ullas and Kshama who have co-authored this book.

Over the years, Shivarama Karanth's incredible creativity, energy and activism earned him many accolades, including eight honorary doctorates and several prestigious national and international awards as listed below. Karanth renounced the Padma Bhushan award in 1975, to protest the imposition of the Emergency by Indira Gandhi.

In 1974, at age seventy-two, Shivarama Karanth left Puttur and returned to settle near his birthplace of Kota. He was active till the very end of his life. Following a stroke, Karanth passed away on 9 December 1997.

## *Honours, awards and accolades received*

1929– Devaraja Bahadur Prize for the book on Indian paintings, *Bharathiya Chitrakale*

1943– Devaraja Bahadur Prize for the novel *Marali Mannige*

1955– President, Kannada Sahitya Sammelana at Mysore

1958– Bronze medal, Le Archive Le International, Stockholm, for research on Yakshagana

1959– Central Sahitya Academy Prize, New Delhi, for the book *Yakshagana Bayalata*

1962– Honorary doctorate, Karnatak University, Dharwad, Karnataka

1962– Honorary doctorate, University of Mysore, Karnataka

1966– Fellowship of the Karnataka State Sahitya Academy

1968– India's Presidential Honour, Padma Bhushan

1973– Honorary fellowship, Central Sangeet Nataka Academy

1975– National Film Award for story and script of the movie *Chomana Dudi*

1976– Honorary doctorate, Meerut University, Uttar Pradesh

1977– Jnanpith Award for the novel *Mookajjiya Kanasugalu*

1979– Karnataka State Sahitya Academy prize for the book *Kala Prapancha*

1982– Japanese Dance Critic's award for Yaksharanga dance performances

1983– Honorary doctorate, Mangalore University, Karnataka

1983– Honorary doctorate, Jabalpur University, Madhya Pradesh

1984– Karnataka State Lalitha Kala Academy prize for the book *Bharathiya Shilpa Kale*

1985– Honorary fellowship, Central Sahitya Academy

1986– Honorary doctorate, World Academy of Arts and Culture, California, US

1989– Campbell Memorial Gold Medal, The Asiatic Society of Bombay

1990– Dadabhai Naoroji Memorial Award

1990– Tulsi Sanman Award of the Madhya Pradesh Government for Yakshagana revival

1991– Paul Harris Fellowship, Rotary International

1992– Fellowship, Ministry of Human Resource Development, for work on Yakshagana

1992– *Pampa Prashashthi* Award, Karnataka government, for the novel *Maimanagala Sulialli*

1992– Indira Gandhi Paryavaran Puraskar, Ministry of Environment and Forests, Government of India

1993– Award of the Justice K.S. Hegde Foundation

1995– Sir M. Visveshvarya Memorial Award, Karnataka Chamber of Commerce and Industry

1996– Honorary membership, Lions International

1996– Honorary membership, Bharathiya Vidya Bhavan

1997– *Desikottam*, Honorary doctorate of Viswa-Bharati University, Shantiniketan, Bengal

1997– *Nadoja*, Honorary doctorate of Kannada University, Hampi, Karnataka

# APPENDIX–2

# POEMS

## *TO DEPARTED HARSHA*

*Leela Karanth*

*(Translated from Kannada by Ajayswarup)*

You left, never to return
I longed for your return

Unfathomed, as you broke the bond
And disappeared from my sight
Detaching, tearing the veil of illusion
My child, you became immortal!

You ...
I longed for your return
As the fog cleared from my mind, I felt your presence
You never went afar,
But stayed close to me
You came and stood so near
Radiantly visible to the mind's eye

Emerging out of my womb
You sucked the nectar from my breast

You are the emotion in my heart
And show up ever in the form of Sai
You also shine in Ullas
You became the light of my life

******************************

# CHERISHED MEMORIES

*Kshama Rau*

When the Sun's rays in the morning
Touched the crystal-like beads of dew
Strung on the great cobwebs between the two trees
Colours of rainbow glistened
It was a magical morning!

After the first rain
In the thick of the night
Fireflies would light up entire tree trunks
In perfect synchrony
In a magical display of lights

When the chikoos ripened in the orchard
As the dark night engulfed Balavana
A pack of jackals cry 'UkkyoUkkyo'
In chorus, from nowhere

I and my brother, when we were small children
Huddled close to our father on the bed at night
Many fantastic stories he told us

Stories of fantasies, of faraway lands and forests
Of rakshasas and rakshasis
Tigers and deer!
We were transported to a land of fantasy

Parrots with cherry red beaks
Winding gracefully up and down
On drumsticks
Pecking at kernels

Brilliant blue kingfisher
Diving deep into the pond
Coming out with a fish

Emerald doves
Whizz past at low height
With their jewel like green wings

Kutur-Kutur of the ring dove
Tak-Tak-Tak sound
Of the golden backed woodpecker
Tapping fiercely at wood
Trin Trio ... the plaintive cry
Of the lapwing
Crying for its lost egg and nest

Visual and Aural
Intertwine forever
Etched in my memory.

# ACKNOWLEDGEMENTS

***To those who made this book possible***

We would like to express our gratitude to the numerous individuals, both living and deceased, as well as to institutions that helped us create *Growing up Karanth*.

We were motivated to embark on this daunting venture by Dr Chiranjiv Singh, a friend and admirer of our late father. Dr Singh, an erudite intellectual and Kannadiga by choice, has been virtually our family member for years. We are also grateful for the moving foreword that he contributed.

Historian Ramachandra Guha has, for many years, actively canvassed the need for recognising Shivarama Karanth's rightful place in the nation's intellectual firmament. We thank him for encouraging us as well as for his eloquent endorsement of the book.

We would also like to express our deep gratitude to the eminent scientist Prof. C.N.R. Rao, technocratic icon N.R. Narayana Murthy, eminent writer and parliamentarian Shashi Tharoor and the well-known novelist Shashi Deshpande for their endorsements.

In the initial stages of this book project, journalists Sugata Srinivasaraju and Rosy Fernandes assisted us in the preparation of several transcripts of interviews they had done with people mentioned in this volume, in English and Kannada respectively. Our friend, psychologist and theatre personality Vijay Padaki offered valuable suggestions on an early draft.

While writing her chapters, Malavika Kapur was assisted by Rajalakshmi Gopala Rao and by Ajayswarup for translating the Kannada poem by Leela Karanth. Kshama Rau was assisted by H. Madhava Bhat and Sanjeeva Suvarna while writing her chapters. Ganashree Kedlaya assisted Ullas Karanth in copyediting the manuscript.

We thank outstanding photographers, Yajna Acharya, Astro Mohan, Sandesh Kadur, Ramnath Chandrasekhar, Vijay Patherphekar, Shekar Dattatri and other friends and family members who helped with some of the images used in the volume. We are also grateful to the Regional Resource Centre of the Manipal Academy of Higher Education and its affiliate, Govinda Pai Research Centre, at MGM College, Udupi, Shivarama Karanth Study Centre at Vivekananda College, Puttur and the Department of Information, Government of Karnataka, for some of the images and information we have used.

We would like to thank our editor Karthik Venkatesh, publisher V.K. Karthika and the production team at Westland who edited, designed, and produced this book so elegantly.

### *To those who enriched our narrative*

In this book we chose to focus on a few key individuals who played important roles in the context of our story. Our narrative draws on our own personal interactions, correspondences, texts and images generously shared by several individuals who are no more. Thus we can only posthumously express our gratitude to Shivarma Karanth, Leela Karanth, Harsha Karanth, Sooryanarayana Karanth, Sumathi Karanth, Padukone Prabhashankar Rao, Vrinda Padukone, Vasantha Sathyashankar, Sunanda Baliga, K.K. Hebbar, Girija Kulal, Someshwar Shyam Sunder, Anandarama Holla, Vasudeva Nayak, Raghu Ram K., Krishna Karanth, Narayana Manjeshwara, Shankari Bhat, Leela Bhat, K.S. Haridas Bhat, Bolanthakody Ishwara Bhat and Dr Chittaranjan Shetty.

For similar support, we also profusely thank the following individuals who are still in touch with us: Prathibha Karanth, M. Ganesh Bhat, Ananda Poojari, Rama Mogera, Gowri Pai, Araty Shetty, Rekha Tiagarajah, Mohandas Bhandari, Svapna Sabnis, Krithi Karanth, Sachindra Karanth, Shantharama Karanth, Aruna Thumbe, Shivasharan Someshwar, Mala Ullas, Vijayalakshmi Rao, Anupama Hegde, Prathibha Shastri, Gundmi Ramesh Aithal, Sanjiva Prasad, Mahesh Padukone, Rekha Rao, Rajni Prasanna, Ranna Hebbar, Jayaprakash Mavinakuli, Rekha Bannadi, K.V. Akshara, Sudhir Vombatkere, Ganapathy Joisa, G.G. Rajendra, Heranje Krishna Bhat, Manorama Bhat, Shyamala Sukumaran, Shubha Raghuram, Vibha Raghuram, Deepthi Sukumaran, Kalpana Tata, Asha Kallianpur, Padaru Mahabaleshwara Bhat and N.G. Mohan.

We note several other individuals who played key roles in the events and times we narrate, but are unfortunately no more with us. We could not write about them for want of specific information as well as constraints of space. These relatives and friends include Venkappa Shetty, Kalladka Narayana Rao, Dr M. Narayana Rao, Menala Seetharama Rai, Mankude Shankaranarayana Rao, Dr Vishwanath and Balayya Sherigar. However, we are most grateful to all of them, and to any others who we may have inadvertantly missed mentioning.

**K. Ullas Karanth**
**Malavika Kapur**
**Kshama Rau**

www.ingramcontent.com/pod-product-compliance
Lightning Source LLC
Chambersburg PA
CBHW061509120726
48001CB00004B/1273